BILLY
SUNDAY

BILLY SUNDAY

SUNDAY

The Man and His Message

By

WILLIAM T. ELLIS

*With revisions and condensation for
present-day readers*

WILLIAM ASHLEY SUNDAY
1863-1935

MOODY PRESS
CHICAGO

ISBN 0-8024-0042-6

29 30 31 32 Printing/LC/Year 88 87

Printed in the United States of America

CONTENTS

5

ONE OF GOD'S TOOLS

I want to be a giant for God—"BILLY" SUNDAY.

HEAVEN OFTEN PLAYS JOKES on earth's worldly-wise, when a shockingly unconventional John the Baptist comes along, who does not follow the prescribed rules in dress, training, methods or message.

In a day full of blatant worldly wisdom, prosperity, churchliness, and a flood of "advanced" theology overwhelming the pulpit, God needed a prophet, to call his people to simple faith and righteousness. A nation was imperiled by luxury, greed, love of pleasure and unbelief. Surely such a day required a great man, learned in all the ways of the world, equipped with the best preparation of American and foreign universities and theological seminaries, a man trained in Church leadership, and approved and honored by the Church. So worldly wisdom decreed. But God laughed and produced, to the scandal of the correct and conventional, "Billy" Sunday, a man from the common people, who, like Lincoln, wore the signs and savor of the soil.

7

That he was God's tool is the first and last word about "Billy" Sunday. He was a "phenomenon" only as God is forever doing the phenomenal, and upsetting men's plans. He was simply a tool of God. For a special work he was the special instrument. God called, and he answered. All the many attempts to "explain" "Billy" Sunday on psychological and sociological grounds fall flat when they ignore the fact the he was a handy man for the Lord's use.

"Billy" Sunday led more persons to make a public confession of discipleship to Jesus Christ than any other man for a century. Approximately three hundred thousand persons, in twenty-five years, took Sunday's hand in token that thenceforth their lives belonged to the Saviour, Jesus Christ.

That amazing statement is too big to be grasped at once. It requires thinking. The huge total needs to be broken up into component parts of living people. Tens of thousands of the men were husbands —hundreds of whom had been separated from their wives and children by sin. In reunited homes, whole families blessed the memory of the man of God who gave them back their husbands and fathers. Other tens of thousands were sons, over many of whom parents had prayed long. It would be hard to convince those mothers, whose sons had been given back to clean living and to Christian service, that there was anything seriously wrong with Mr. Sunday's language or methods or theology. Businessmen who found that a Sunday revival meant the paying up of the bad bills of old customers were ready to approve a man whose work restored integrity in commercial relations.

Every conceivable type of humanity was included in that total of over a quarter of a million of converts. The college professor, the prosperous businessman, the eminent politician, the farmer, the lawyer, the editor, the doctor, the author, the athlete, the "man about town," the criminal, the drunkard, the society woman, the college student, the workingman, the school boy and girl—the whole gamut of life was covered by the stream of humanity that "hit the sawdust trail"—a phrase which chilled the marrow of the theological seminaries. But the trail led Home to the Father's House.

He, above all others of his time, broke through the thick wall of indifference which separated the church from the world. The church's problem was how to smash, or even to crack, the partition which shut off the world from the church.

"Billy" Sunday did it. He set all sorts and conditions of men to talking about religion. In the lowest dive in New York's "Tenderloin" or in San Francisco's "Barbary Coast," the name " 'Billy' "Sunday," was recognized, and denizens were ready to discuss the man and his message. Stand before a session of the American Philosophical Society and pronounce the words, "Billy" Sunday, and every one of the learned savants present would be able to talk about the man, even though few of them knew who won last season's baseball championship or who held the world's ring championship.

That was a feat of magnitude. All levels of society were made aware of "Billy" Sunday and his gospel. When the evangelist went to New York for an evening address, early in the year 1914, the throngs were so great that the police were surprised by surging thousands. Mr. Sunday himself could not obtain admittance to the meeting for more than half an hour. Andrew Carnegie could not get into the hall that bears his name. Probably a greater number of persons tried to hear the evangelist that night than were gathered in all the churches of greater New York combined on the preceding Sunday night. To turn thousands of persons away from his meetings was a common experience. More than ten thousand, mostly men, tried in vain to get into the overcrowded Scranton tabernacle at a single session.

That generation had not seen a great city shaken by the gospel until "Billy" Sunday went to Pittsburgh. The report was unanimously given by the press, preachers and businessmen. Literally that whole city was stirred to its sluggish depths by the Sunday campaign. No baseball series or political campaign ever moved the community so deeply. Everywhere one went the talk was of "Billy" Sunday and his meetings. From the bell boys in the hotels to the wealthy in the Duquesne Club, from the workmen in the mills and the girls in the stores to the women in exclusive gatherings, Sunday was conversation. Philadelphia more than duplicated this experience.

Day by day, all the newspapers in that city gave pages to the Sunday meetings. The sermons were fully reported. No other topic had received such full attention for so long a time at the hands of the press. The issues of the papers were subscribed for by persons in all parts of the world. Men and women were converted who never heard the sound of the evangelist's voice. This series of Philadelphia meetings, more than anything else in his experience, impressed the power of Sunday upon the metropolitan centers of the nation at large; the country folk had long before learned of him.

Any tabulation of Mr. Sunday's influence must give a high place to the fact that he made good press "copy": he put religion on the front pages of the dailies; and made it an issue with the millions.

All of this proved the popular interest in vital,

contemporaneous religion. Men's ears were dulled by the "shop talk" of the pulpit. They were weary of the worn platitudes of professional piety. Nobody cared for the language of Canaan, in which many ministers, with reverence for the dead past, tried to envelope the living truths of the Gospel, as if they were mummies. In the colloquial tongue of the common people, Jesus first proclaimed His gospel, and "the common people heard him gladly." Many of the learned and aristocratic ecclesiastics of his day were scandalized by Sunday's free and popular way of putting things, by his stories, and by his disregard for the precedents of the schools. Whatever else may be said about "Billy" Sunday's much-discussed forms of speech, this point was clear, and denied by nobody: he made himself and his message clearly understood by all classes of people. However much one might disagree with him, nobody failed to catch his meaning. He harnessed the common words of the street to the chariot of divine truth.

College students liked him as much as did farmers and mechanics. In a single day's work at the University of Pennsylvania, when thousands of students crowded his meetings, and gave reverent, absorbed attention to his message, several hundred of them openly dedicated their lives to Christ, and publicly grasped his hand. Dr. John R. Mott, one of the world's greatest student leaders, once said: "'You cannot fool a great body of students. They get a man's measure. If he is genuine, they know it, and if he is not, they quickly find it out. Their devotion to Mr. Sunday is very significant."

His appeal was to the mass of the people. The housekeepers who seldom ventured away from their homes, the mechanics who did not go to church, the "men about town" who professed a cynical disdain for religion, the "down and outs," the millionaires, the society women, the business and professional men, the young fellows who felt "too big" to go to Sunday school—all these, and scores of other types, were found night after night in the barn-like, wooden tabernacles which were always erected for the meetings.

CHAPTER 2

UP FROM THE SOIL

If you want to drive the devil out of the world, hit him with a cradle instead of a crutch—"BILLY" SUNDAY.

S UNDAY MUST BE ACCEPTED as an American type before he can be understood. He was of the average American sort. He was one of the "folks." He had more points of resemblance to the common people than he had of difference from them. His mind was their mind. The keenness of the average American was his in an increased degree. He had the saving sense of humor which marked the West. The extravagances and recklessnesses of his speech would be incredible to a Britisher. Americans understood them.

Sunday was not over-fastidious. He was not made of special porcelain clay, but of the same red soil as the rest of us. He knew the barnyards of the farm better than the drawing rooms of the rich. The normal, everyday Americanism of this son of the Middle West, whom the nation knew as "Billy"

Sunday, is to be insisted upon if he is to be understood.

Early apprenticed to hardship and labor, he had a sympathy with the life of the toiling people which mere imagination cannot give. His knowledge of the American crowd was sure and complete because he was one of them. He understood the life of everyday folk because that had always been his life. While he had obvious natural ability, sharpened on the grindstone of varied experience, his perceptions and his viewpoints were those of the normal American. As he had seen something of life on many levels, and knew city ways as well as country usages, he never lost his bearings as to what sort of people made up the bulk of his country. To them his sermons were addressed. Because he struck this medium level of common conduct and thought, it was easy for those in all the levels of American life to comprehend him.

"Horse sense" was Sunday's to an eminent degree. Because he was "rich in saving common sense," Sunday understood the people and trusted them to understand him. His most earnest defenders from the beginning of his public life were the rank and file of the common people. His critics were from the extreme edges of society—the scholar, or the man whose business was hurt by righteousness.

The life of William A. Sunday covered the period of American history from the Civil War to 1935. He never saw his father, for he was born the third son of pioneer parents on November 19, 1862, four months after his father had enlisted as a private in Company E, Twenty-third Iowa Infantry Volunteers, from which he never returned.

There is nothing remarkable to record as to the family. They were one with the type of the middle-western Americans who wrested that empire from the wilderness, and counted poverty honorable. In those mutually helpful, splendidly independent days, Democracy came to its flower.

Real patriotism is always purchased at a high price; none pay more dearly for wartime loyalty than the women who send their husbands and sons to the front. Mrs. Sunday bade her husband answer the call of his country as only a brave woman could do. He went to the service and sacrifices which soon ended in an unmarked grave. Four months after she had bidden farewell to her husband, she bade welcome to his son. To this third child she gave the name of her absent husband.

The mother's dreams of the returning soldier's delight in his namesake child were soon disspelled by the tidings that Private William Sunday had died of disease contracted in service, at Patterson, Missouri, on December 22, 1862. A little more than a month later the boy was born who was to lift the name out of the obscurity of the hosts of those who gave "the last full measure of devotion" to their nation.

Then the mother was called upon to take up that heaviest of all burdens of patriotism—the rearing of an orphan family in a home of dire poverty. The three children in the Sunday home at Ames, Iowa— Roy, Edward and William—were unwitting participants in another aspect of war, the lot of soldiers' orphans. For years, Mrs. Sunday, was able to keep her family together under the roof of the two-roomed, log cabin which they called home. In those early days their grandfather, Squire Corey, was of unmeasured help in providing for and training the three orphan boys.

Experience is a school teacher who carries a rod, as Sunday could well testify. He earned life's fundamental lessons in the school of poverty and toil. To the part which his mother played in shaping his life and ideals he has borne eloquent tribute on many platforms. When the youngest son was twelve years old, he and his older brother were sent off to the Soldiers' Orphanage at Glenwood, Iowa. Later they were transferred to the Davenport Orphanage, which they left in June of 1876, making two years spent in the orphanages. Concerning this experience Sunday says:

"I was bred and born in Iowa. I am a rube of the rubes. I am a hayseed of the hayseeds, and the malodors of the barnyard are on me yet. It beats Pinadu and Colgate. I have greased my hair with goose grease and blacked my boots with stove blacking. I have wiped my old proboscis with a gunny-sack towel; I have drunk coffee out of my saucer, and I have eaten with my knife; I have said 'done it,' when I should have said 'did it,' and I 'have saw' when I should 'have seen,' and I expect to go to Heaven. I have crept and crawled out from the university of poverty and hard knocks, and have taken postgraduate courses.

"My father went to the war four months before I was born. I have butted and fought and struggled since I was six years old. That's one reason why I wear that little red, white and blue button. I know all about the dark and seamy side of life, and if ever a man fought hard, I have fought hard for everything I have ever gained.

"The wolf scratched at the cabin door and finally mother said: 'Boys, I am going to send you to the Soldiers' Orphans' Home.' At Ames, Iowa, we had to wait for the train, and we went to a little hotel, and they came about one o'clock and said: 'Get ready for the train.'

"I looked into mother's face. Her eyes were red,

her hair was disheveled. I said: 'What's the matter, Mother?' All the time Ed and I slept mother had been praying. We went to the train; she put one arm about me and the other about Ed and sobbed as if her heart would break. People walked by and looked at us, but they didn't say a word.

"Why? They didn't know, and if they had they wouldn't have cared. Mother knew; she knew that for years she wouldn't see her boys. We got into the train and said, 'Good-by, Mother,' as the train pulled out. We reached Council Bluffs. It was cold and we turned up our coats and shivered. We saw the hotel and went up and asked the woman for something to eat. She said: 'What's your name?'

" 'My name is William Sunday, and this is my brother Ed.'

" 'Where are you going?'

" 'Going to the Soldiers' Orphans' Home at Glenwood.'

"She wiped her tears and said: 'My husband was a soldier and never came back. He wouldn't turn any one away and I wouldn't turn you boys away.' She put her arms about us and said: 'Come on in.' She gave us our breakfast and our dinner, too. There wasn't any train going out on the 'Q' until afternoon. We saw a freight train standing there, so we climbed into the caboose.

"The conductor came along and said: 'Where's your money or ticket?'

" 'Ain't got any.'

" 'I'll have to put you off.'

"We commenced to cry. My brother handed him a letter of introduction to the superintendent of the orphans' home. The conductor read it, and handed it back as the tears rolled down his cheeks. Then he said: 'Just sit still, boys. It won't cost a cent to ride on my train.'

"It's only twenty miles from Council Bluffs to Glenwood, and as we rounded the curve the conductor said: 'There it is on the hill.'

"I want to say to you that one of the brightest pictures that hangs upon the walls of my memory is the recollection of the days when as a little boy, out in the log cabin on the frontier of Iowa, I knelt by Mother's side.

"I went back to the old farm some years ago. The scenes had changed. Faces I had known and loved had long since turned to dust. Fingers that used to turn the pages of the Bible were obliterated and the old trees beneath which we boys used to play and swing had been felled. I stood and thought. The man became a child again and the long weary night of sin and of hardships became as though they never had been.

"Once more with my gun on my shoulder and my favorite dog trailing at my heels I walked through the pathless wood and sat on the old familiar logs and stumps. As I sat and listened to the wild, weird harmonies of nature, a vision of the past opened. The squirrel from the limb of the tree barked defiantly and I threw myself into an interrogation point, and when the gun cracked, the squirrel fell at my feet. I grabbed him and ran home to throw him down and receive compliments for my skill as a marksman. I saw the tapestry of the evening fall. I heard the lowing herds and saw them wind slowly o'er the lea and I listened to the tinkling bells that lulled the distant fowl. Once more I heard the shouts of childish glee. Once more Mother drew the trundle bed out from under the larger one, and we boys, kneeling down, shut our eyes and, clasping our little hands, said: 'Now, I lay me down to sleep; I pray the Lord, my soul to keep. If I should die before I wake, I pray thee,

Lord, my soul to take. And this I ask for Jesus' sake,
Amen.'

> Backward, turn backward, O time in thy flight,
> Make me a child again, just for tonight,
> Mother, come back from that echoless shore,
> Take me again to your heart as of yore.
> Into the old cradle I'm longing to creep,
> Rock me to sleep, Mother, rock me to sleep.

"I stood beneath the old oak tree and it seemed to carry on a conversation with me. It seemed to say:

"'Hello Bill. Is that you?'

"'Yes, it's I, old tree.'

"'Well, you've got a bald spot on the top of your head.'

"'Yes, I know, old tree.'

"'Won't you climb up and sit on my limbs as you used to?'

"'No, I haven't got time now. I'd like to, though, awfully well.'

"'Don't go, Bill. Don't you remember the old swing you made?'

"'Yes, I remember; but I've got to go.'

"'Say Bill, don't you remember when you tried to play George Washington and the cherry tree and almost cut me down? That's the scar you made, but it's almost covered over now.'

"'Yes, I remember all, but I haven't time to stay.'

"'Are you comin' back, Bill?'

"'I don't know, but I'll never forget you.'

"Then the old apple tree seemed to call me and I said: 'I haven't time to wait, old apple tree.'

> I want to go back to the orchard,
>   The orchard that used to be mine,
> The apples are reddening and filling
>   The air with their wine.

I want to run on through the pasture
   And let down the dusty old bars,
I want to find you there still waiting,
   Your eyes like the twin stars.
Oh, nights, you are weary and dreary,
   And days, there is something you lack;
To the farm in the valley,
   I want to go back.

"I tell it to you with shame, I stretched the elastic bands of my mother's love until I thought they would break. I went far into the dark and the wrong until I ceased to hear her prayers or her pleadings. I forgot her face, and I went so far that it seemed to me that one more step and the bands of her love would break and I would be lost. But, thank God, friends, I never took that last step. Little by little I yielded to the tender memories and recollections of my mother; little by little I was drawn away from the yawning abyss, and one dark and stormy night in Chicago, I groped my way out of darkness into the arms of Jesus Christ and I fell on my knees and cried, 'God be merciful to me a sinner!'"

Of formal education the boy Sunday had but little. He went to school intermittently, like most of his playmates, but he did get into high school, though he was never graduated. Early in life he began to work for his living, even before he went off to the Soldiers' Orphanage. Concerning these periods of early toil he says:

"When I was about fourteen years old, I made application for the position of janitor in a school.

"I used to get up at two o'clock, and there were fourteen stoves to which coal had to be carried. I had to keep the fire up and keep up my studies and sweep the floors. I got twenty-five dollars a month salary. One day I got a check for my salary and I went right down to the bank to get it cashed.

Right in front of me was another fellow with a check to be cashed, and he shoved his in, and I came along and shoved my check in, and I was handed forty dollars. My check called for twenty-five dollars. I called on a friend of mine who was a lawyer in Kansas City and told him: 'Frank, what do you think, Jay King handed me forty dollars and my check only called for twenty-five dollars.' He said, 'Bill, if I had your luck, I would buy a lottery ticket.' But I said, 'The fifteen dollars is not mine.' He said, 'Don't be a chump. If you were shy ten dollars and you went back you would not get it, and if they hand out fifteen dollars, don't be a fool, keep it.'

"Well, he had some drag with me and influenced me. I was fool enough to keep it, and I took it and bought a suit of clothes. I can see that suit now; it was a kind of brown with a little green in it and I thought I was the goods. That was the first suit of store clothes I had ever had, and I bought that suit and I had twenty-five dollars left.

"Years afterward I said: 'I ought to be a Christian,' and I got on my knees to pray, and the Lord seemed to touch me on the back and say: 'Bill, you owe that Farmers' Bank fifteen dollars with interest.' I said: 'Lord, the Bank don't know that I got that fifteen dollars,' and the Lord said: 'I know it.' So I struggled along for years, probably like some of you, trying to be decent and honest and right some wrong that was in my life, and every time I got down to pray the Lord would say, 'Fifteen dollars with interest, Nevada County, Iowa; fifteen dollars, Bill.' So years afterward I sent that money back, enclosed a check, wrote a letter and acknowledged it. I have the peace of God from that day to this, and I have never swindled anyone out of a dollar."

There are other kinds of education besides those which award students a sheepskin at the end of a stated term. "Billy" Sunday's school was a diversity of work, where he came face to face with the actualities of life. He early had to shift for himself. He learned the priceless lesson of how to work, regardless of what the particular task might be, whether it was scrubbing floors (he was an expert scrubber of floors!), or preaching a sermon to twenty thousand persons. He had a long hard drill in working under authority: that is why he was able to exercise authority like a major-general. Because personally he experienced, with all of the sensitiveness of an American small boy, the bitter injustice of overwork and underpay under an oppressive taskmaster, he was a voice for the toilers of the world. In this same diversified school of industry he learned the lesson of thoroughness which was echoed by every spike in his tabernacle and every gesture in his sermons. A person like Mr. Sunday could not have come from a conventional educational course. It needed this hard school to make a hardy man.

It was while a youth in Marshalltown, Iowa, playing baseball on the lots, that Sunday came to his own. Captain A. C. Anson, the famous leader of the Chicago "White Sox" chanced to see this youth of twenty, whose phenomenal base running had made him a local celebrity. It was no new experience for Sunday to be a center of public interest. He had known this since boyhood. The local baseball "hero" was as big a figure in the eyes of his own particular circle as ever a great evangelist gets to be in the view of the world. Because his ears early became accustomed to the huzzas of the crowd, Sunday's head was not turned by much of the foolish adulation which was his when he became an evangelist.

A level head, a quick eye, and a body which was such a finely trained instrument that it could meet all drawings upon it, was part of Sunday's inheritance from his life on the baseball diamond.

Most successful baseball players enter the major leagues by a succession of steps. With Sunday it was quite otherwise. Because he fell under the personal eye of "Pop" Anson he was transferred directly from the fields of Marshalltown, Iowa, to the great park of the Chicago team. That was in 1883, when Sunday was not yet twenty-one years of age. His mind was still formative—and his entrance into the larger field of baseball trained him to think in broad terms. It widened his horizon and made him reasonably indifferent to the comments of crowds.

A better equipment for the work he was to do could not have been found; for above all else Sunday "played ball." While others discussed methods and bewailed conditions he kept the game going. Such a volume of criticism as no other evangelist, within the memory of living men, ever received, fell harmless, because he did not stop to argue with the umpire, but kept on the job.

There is no call for tears over the early experiences of Sunday. His life was normal; no different from that of tens of thousands of other American boys. He himself was in no wise a phenomenon. He was possessed of no special abilities or inclinations. He came to his preaching gift only after years of experience in Christian work. It is clear that a divine Providence utilized the very ordinariness of his life and training to make him an ambassador to the common people.

CHAPTER 3

A BASEBALL "STAR"

Don't get chesty over success—"BILLY" SUNDAY.

SOMETIMES THE PREACHER tells his people what a great journalist he might have been, or what a successful businessman, had he not entered the ministry; but usually his hearers never would have suspected it if he had not told them. "Billy" Sunday's eminence as a baseball player was not a shadow cast backward from his later pre-eminence. His success as a preacher gained luster from his distinction as a baseball player; his fame as a baseball player was kept alive by his work as an evangelist.

All the world of baseball enthusiasts of that day knew "Billy" Sunday to be the speediest base runner and the most daring base stealer in the whole fraternity. Wherever he went veteran devotees of the national game recalled times they saw him play; sporting periodicals and sporting pages of newspapers carried reminiscences from baseball "fans" of the triumphs of the evangelist on the diamond.

A side light on the reality of his religion while engaged in professional baseball is the fact that sports writers always spoke of him with pride and loyalty, and his old baseball associates would go frequently to hear him preach.

Now baseball in Marshalltown and baseball in Chicago had not exactly the same standards. The recruit had to be drilled. He struck out the first thirteen times he went to bat. He never became a superior batter, but he could always throw straight and hard. At first he was inclined to take too many chances and his judgment was rather unsafe. One baseball writer said: "Sunday probably caused more wide throws than any other player the game has ever known, because of his specialty of going down to first like a streak of lightning. When he hit the ball, infielders yelled 'hurry it up.' The result was that they often threw them away." He was the acknowledged champion sprinter of the National League. This once led to a match race with Arlie Latham, who held like honors in the American League. Sunday won by fifteen feet.

Sunday was the sort of figure the bleachers liked. He was always eager—sometimes too eager—to "take a chance." What was a one-base hit for another man was usually good for two bases for him. His slides and stolen bases were adventures beloved of the "fans"—the spice of the game. He also was apt in retort to the comments from the bleachers, but always good-natured. The crowds liked him, as did his teammates.

Sunday was a man's man. His tabernacle audiences resembled baseball crowds in the proportion of men present. Sunday spent five years on the old Chicago team, mostly playing right or center field. He was the first man in the history of baseball to circle the bases in fourteen seconds. He ran a hundred yards from a standing start in ten seconds flat. Speed had always been his one distinction. As a lad of thirteen, in the Fourth of July games at Ames, he won a prize of three dollars in a foot race, a feat recalled with pleasure.

Speed is a phase of baseball that, being clear to all eyes, appeals to the bleachers. So it came about that Sunday was soon a baseball "hero" analogous to "Ty" Cobb or "Home-Run" Baker, or "Christy" Mathewson. He told the story of one famous play, on the day after his conversion:

"That afternoon we played the old Detroit club. We were neck and neck for the championship. That club had Thompson, Richardson, Rowe, Dunlap, Hanlon and Bennett, and they could play ball.

"I was playing right field. Mike Kelly was catching and John G. Clarkson was pitching. He was as fine a pitcher as ever crawled into uniform. There are some pitchers today, O'Toole, Bender, Wood, Mathewson, Johnson, Marquard, but I do not believe any one of them stood in the class with Clarkson.

"We had two men out and they had a man on second and one on third and Bennett, their old catcher, was at bat. Charley had three balls and two strikes on him. Charley couldn't hit a high ball: but he could kill them when they went about his knee.

"I 'hollered' to Clarkson: 'One more and we got 'em.'

"You know every pitcher puts a hole in the ground where he puts his foot when he is pitching. John stuck his foot in the hole and he went clean to the ground. Oh, he could make 'em dance. He could throw overhanded, and the ball would go down and up. He is the only man I have seen do that. That ball would go by so fast that the batter could feel the thermometer drop two degrees as she whizzed by. John went clean down, and as he went to throw the ball his right foot slipped and the ball went low instead of high.

"I saw Charley swing hard and heard the bat hit the ball with a terrific boom. Bennett had smashed the ball on the nose. I saw the ball rise in the air and knew that it was going clear over my head.

"I could judge within ten feet of where the ball would light. I turned my back to the ball and ran.

"The field was crowded with people; I yelled, 'Stand back!' and that crowed opened as the Red Sea opened for the rod of Moses. I ran on, and as I ran I made a prayer; it wasn't theological, either. I said, 'God, if you ever helped mortal man, help me to get that ball, and you haven't very much time to make up your mind, either.' I ran and jumped over the bench and stopped.

"I thought I was close enough to catch it. I looked back and saw it was going over my head. I jumped and shoved out my left hand and the ball hit it and stuck. At the rate I was going the momentum carried me on and I fell under the feet of a team of horses. I jumped up with the ball in my hand. Up came Tom Johnson. Tom used to be mayor of Cleveland. He's dead now.

" 'Here is $10, Bill. Buy yourself the best hat in Chicago. That catch won me $1,500. Tomorrow go and buy yourself the best suit of clothes you can find in Chicago.'

"An old Methodist minister said to me a few years ago, 'Why, William, you didn't take the $10, did you?' I said, 'You bet your life I did.' "

For most of his baseball career Sunday was an out-and-out Christian. He had been converted in 1887, after four years of membership on the Chicago team. He had worked at his religion; his teammates knew his Christianity for the real thing. On Sundays, because of his eminence as a baseball player, he was in great demand for Y. M. C. A. talks. Sporting papers all alluded frequently to his religious interests and activities. Because of his Christian scruples he refused to play baseball on Sunday. During the four years of his experience as a Christian member of the baseball profession it might have been clear to anybody who cared to study the situation that the young man's interest in religion was steadily deepening and that he was headed toward some form of avowedly Christian service.

"I had a three-year contract with Philadelphia. I said to God: 'Now if you want me to quit playing ball and go into evangelistic work, then you get my release,' and so I left it with God to get my release before March 25, and I would take that as an evidence that He wanted me to quit playing ball.

"On March 17, St. Patrick's day—I shall never forget it—I was leading a meeting and received a letter from Colonel Rogers, president of the Philadelphia club, stating I could have my release.

"In came Jim Hart, of the Cincinnati team, and up on the platform and pulled out a contract. He said: 'Bill, sign up!' But I said, 'No!' I told him that I told God if he wanted me to quit playing ball to get my release before March 25 and I would quit.

"There I was up against it. I went around to some of my friends and some said: 'Take it!' Others said, 'Stick to your promise.' I asked my father-in-law about it, and he said, 'You are a blank fool if you don't take it.' I went home and went to bed, but could not sleep, and prayed that night until five o'clock, when I seemed to get the thing straight and said, 'No, sir, I will not do it.'

"I went to work for the Y. M. C. A. and had a very hard time of it. It was during those hard times that I hardly had enough to pay my house rent, but I stuck to my promise."

It was in March of 1891 that Sunday made the decision which marked the parting of the ways for him. He abandoned baseball forever as a profession, although not as an interest, and entered upon definite religious work. He accepted a position in the Chicago Y. M. C. A. as a subordinate secretary at $83.33 per month—and sometimes this was six months overdue.

The stuff of which the young man's moral character was made is revealed by the fact that he deliberately rejected a fat baseball contract in order to serve Christ at a personal sacrifice.

Doubtless there were many who thought this ending of a conspicuous baseball career an anticlimax, even as the flight of Moses into the wilderness of Sinai apparently spelled defeat. Out of such defeats and sacrifices grow victories that best serve the world and most honor God.

CHAPTER 4

A CURBSTONE RECRUIT

You've got to sign your own Declaration of Independence before you can celebrate your Fourth of July victory—"BILLY" SUNDAY.

NOBODY THIS SIDE OF HEAVEN can tell to whom the credit belongs for any great life or great work. But we may be reasonably sure that the unsung and unknown women of the earth have a large part in every achievement worth while.

Mrs. Clark, saintly wife of Colonel Clark, the devoted founder of the Pacific Garden Rescue Mission in Chicago, is one of that host of women who, like the few who followed Jesus in His earthly ministry, have served in lowly, inconspicuous ways, doing small tasks from a great love. Night after night, with a consecration which never flagged, she labored in the gospel for a motley crowd of men and women, mostly society's flotsam and jetsam, many of whom found this hospitable mission building the last fort this side of destruction.

A single visit to a downtown rescue mission is romantic, picturesque and somewhat of an adventure—a sort of sanctified slumming trip. Far different to spend night after night, regardless of weather or personal feelings, in coming to close grips with sin-sodden men and women! A sickening share of the number are merely seeking shelter or lodging or food. Sin's wages are not sufficient to live upon, and they turn to the mercy of Christianity for succor. Never to be cast down by unworthiness or ingratitude, to keep a heart of hope in face of successive failures, and to rejoice with a shepherd's joy over the one rescued—this is the spirit of the consecrated rescue-mission worker.

Such a woman was Mrs. Clark, spiritual mother to a multitude of redeemed men. Of all the trophies which she has laid at the feet of her Lord, the redemption of "Billy" Sunday seems to human eyes the brightest. For it was this woman who persuaded him to accept Christ as his Saviour: he whose hand has led perhaps a quarter of a million persons to the foot of the Cross was himself led thither by this saintly woman.

When we contemplate the relation of that one humble rescue mission in Chicago, the monument of a businessman's consecration to Christ, to the scores of Sunday tabernacles over the land; when we connect the streams of penitents on the "saw-dust trail" with that one young man of twenty-five going forward up the aisle of the mission room, we realize afresh that God uses many workers to carry on his one work. Though Paul may plant and Apollos water, it is God alone who gives the increase.

It was one evening in the fall of 1887 that Sunday, with five of his baseball teammates, sat on the curbstone of Van Buren Street and listened to the music and testimonies of a band of workers from the Pacific Garden Rescue Mission. The deeps of sentiment inherited from a Christian mother, and the memories of a Christian home, were stirred in the breast of one of the men. Sunday accepted the invitation of a worker to visit the mission. Moved by the testimonies which he heard, he went again and again; and at length, after conversation and prayer with Mrs. Clark, he made the great decision which committed him to the Christian life.

Sunday's own story of his conversion is one of the most thrilling of the evangelist's messages. It is a human document, a leaf in that great book of Christian evidences which God is still writing.

"Twenty-seven years ago I walked down a street in Chicago in company with some ball players who were famous in this world—some of them are dead now—and we went into a saloon. It was Sunday afternoon and we got tanked up and then went and sat down on a corner. I never go by that street without thanking God for saving me. It was a vacant lot at that time. We sat down on a curbing. Across the street a company of men and women were playing on instruments—horns, flutes and slide trombones—and the others were singing the gospel hymns that I used to hear my mother sing back in the log cabin in Iowa and back in the old church where I used to go to Sunday school.

"God painted on the canvas of my recollection and memory a vivid picture of the scenes of other days and other faces.

"Many have long since turned to dust. I sobbed and sobbed, and a young man stepped out and said: 'We are going down to the Pacific Garden Mission. Won't you come down to the mission? I am sure you will enjoy it. You can hear drunkards tell how they have been saved and girls tell how they have been saved from the red-light district.'

"I arose and said to the boys, 'I'm through, I am

going to Jesus Christ. We've come to the parting of the ways.' Some of them laughed and some of them mocked me; one of them gave me encouragement; others never said a word.

"I turned and left that little group on the corner and walked to the little mission and fell on my knees and staggered out of sin and into the arms of the Saviour.

"After that night at the mission I had to get out to the ball park and practice. Every morning at ten o'clock we had to be out there. I never slept that night. I was afraid of the horselaugh that gang would give me because I had taken my stand for Jesus Christ.

"I walked down to the old ball grounds. I will never forget it. I slipped my key into the wicket gate and the first man to meet me after I got inside was Mike Kelly.

"Up came Mike Kelly; he said: 'Bill, I'm proud of you! Religion is not my long suit, but I'll help you all I can.' Up came Anson, the best ball player that ever played the game; Pfeffer, Clarkson, Flint, Jimmy McCormick, Burns, Williamson and Dalrymple. There wasn't a fellow in that gang who knocked; every fellow had a word of encouragement for me.

"Mike Kelly was one of the men I left there on the corner. Mike was sold to Boston for $10,000. Mike got half of the purchase price. He came up to me and showed me a check for $5,000. John L. Sullivan, the champion fighter, went around with a subscription paper and the boys raised over $12,000 to buy Mike a house.

"They gave Mike a deed to the house and they had $1,500 left and gave him a certificate of deposit for that.

"His salary for playing with Boston was $4,700 a

a year. At the end of that season Mike had spent the $5,000 purchase price and the $4,700 he received as salary and the $1,500 they gave him and had a mortgage on the house. When he died in Pennsylvania they went around with a subscription to get money enough to put him in the ground. Each club, twelve in all, in the two leagues gave a month a year to his wife. Mike sat here on the corner with me years ago, when I said, "Good-by, boys, I'm going to Jesus Christ.'

"Frank Flint, our old catcher, was another of the boys I left there on the corner when I went to Christ. Frank caught for nineteen years, drew $3,200 a year on an average. He caught before they had chest protectors, masks and gloves. He caught barehanded. Every bone in the ball of his hand was broken. You never saw such a hand! Every bone in his face was broken, and his nose and cheek bones, and the shoulder and ribs had all been broken. He got to drinking, his home was broken up and he went to 'the dogs.'

"I've seen old Frank Flint sleeping on a table in a stale beer joint and I've turned my pockets inside out and said, "You're welcome to it, old pal.' He drank on and on, and one day in winter he staggered out of a stale beer joint and stood on a corner, and was seized with a fit of coughing. The blood streamed out of his nose, mouth and eyes. Down the street came a wealthy woman. She took one look and said, 'My God, is it you, Frank?' His wife came up and kissed him.

"She called two policemen and a cab and started with him to her boarding house. They broke speed regulations. She called the best physicians and they listened to the beating of his heart, one, two, three, four, five, six, seven, eight, nine, ten eleven, twelve, and the doctors said, 'He will be dead in about four hours.' She told them to tell him what they had told her. She said, 'Frank, the end is near,' and he said, 'Send for Bill.'

"They telephoned and I went. He said: "There's nothing in the life of years ago I care for now. I can hear the bleachers cheer when I make a hit that wins the game. But there is nothing that can help me now; and if the umpire calls me out now, won't you say a few words over me, Bill?" He struggled as he had years ago on the diamond, when he tried to reach Home, but the great Umpire of the universe called, 'You're out!' and waved him to the 'club house,' and the great gladiator of the diamond was no more.

"He sat on the street corner with me, drunk, twenty-seven years ago in Chicago, when I said, 'Good-by, boys, I'm through.'

"Did they win the game of life or did Bill?"

CHAPTER 5

PLAYING THE NEW GAME

It is not necessary to be in a big place to do big things—"BILLY" SUNDAY.

IF BILLY SUNDAY had not been an athlete he would not have been the physical marvel in the pulpit that he was; if he had not been reared in the ranks of the plain people he would not have possessed the vocabulary and insight into life which were essential parts of his equipment. If he had not served a long apprenticeship to toil he would not have displayed his pitiless industry; if he had not been a cog in the machinery of organized baseball, with wide travel and much experience of men, he would not have been able to perfect the amazing organization of his evangelistic campaigns. If he had not been a member and elder of a Presbyterian church he could not have resisted the religious vagaries which led so many evangelists and immature Christian workers astray; if he had not been trained in three years of Y. M. C. A. service he would not have been the flaming and insistent protagonist of personal work that he was. If he had not been converted definitely and consciously and quickly in a rescue mission he could not have preached his gospel of immediate conversion.

All of which is another way of saying that Sunday was trained in God's school. God prepared the man for the work He was preparing for him. Only by such uncommon training could this unique messenger of the gospel have been produced. Over and over again he urged that instead of railing at what we have not enjoyed, we should magnify what we already possess. The shepherd's rod of Moses, rightly wielded, may be mightier than a king's scepter.

As we approach the development of the unique work of "Billy" Sunday, we must reckon with those forces which developed his personality. We must trace the steps which led him into his activity. For he went forward *a step at a time.*

He followed the rule of the rescue mission: the saved should say so. At the very beginning he began to bear testimony to his new faith. Wherever opportunity offered he spoke a good word for Jesus Christ. In many towns and cities his testimony was heard in those early days; and there was not a follower of the baseball game who did not know that "Billy" Sunday was a Christian.

The convert who does not join a church is likely soon to be in a bad way. Sunday early united with the Jefferson Park Presbyterian Church, Chicago. He went into religious activity with all the ardor that he displayed on the baseball field. He attended the Christian Endeavor society, prayer-meeting and the midweek church service. This is significant; it is usually the church members who are faithful at the midweek prayer meetings who are the vital force in a congregation.

Other rewards than spiritual awaited Sunday at the prayer meeting; there he met Helen A. Thompson, the young woman who subsequently became his wife. Between the meeting and the marriage altar there were various obstacles to be overcome. Another suitor was an obstacle, and besides, Miss Thompson's father did not take kindly to the idea of a professional baseball player as a possible son-in-law, for he had old-fashioned, Scottish notions of things. "Love conquers all," and in September, 1888, the young couple were married, taking their wedding trip by going on circuit with the baseball team.

Mrs. Sunday's influence upon her husband was extraordinary. He was a devoted husband, of the American type, and with his ardent loyalty to his wife had complete confidence in her judgment. She was his "man of affairs." Her Scottish heritage endowed her with the prudent qualities of that race, and she was the business manager of Mr. Sunday's campaigns. She it was who held her generous, careless husband down to a realization of the practicalities of life.

He made no important decisions without consulting her. She traveled with him nearly all of the time, attending his meetings and watching over his work and his personal needs like a mother. In addition Mrs. Sunday did yeoman service in the evangelistic campaigns.

The helplessness of the evangelist without his wife was almost ludicrous: he disliked to settle any question, whether it was an acceptance of an invitation from a city, or the employment of an additional worker, without Mrs. Sunday's counsel. Frequently he turned vexing problems over to her, and accepted her decision, without looking into the matter himself.

Four children—Helen, George, William and Paul —were born to the Sundays. The Sunday home was in Winona Lake, Indiana. When Mrs. Sunday was absent with her husband, the two younger children were left in the care of a trusted helper. The evangelist himself was home for only a short period each summer.

Mrs. Sunday was the deciding factor in determining her husband to abandon baseball for religious work. A woman of real Scottish piety, in the time of decision she chose the better part. Her husband had been addressing Y. M. C. A. meetings, Sunday schools and Christian Endeavor societies. He was undeniably a poor speaker. No prophet could have foreseen the master of platform art in the stammering, stumbling young man whose only excuse for addressing public meetings was the eagerness of men to hear the celebrated baseball player's story. His speech was merely his testimony, as required of all mission converts.

If Sunday could not talk well on his feet he could handle individual men. It was his aptness in dealing with men that led the Chicago Young Men's Christian Association to offer him an assistant secretaryship in the department of religious work. It is significant that the baseball player went into the Y. M. C. A. not as a physical director but in the distinctively spiritual sphere. He refused an invitation to become physical director; his religious zeal from the first outshone his physical prowess.

Those three years of work in the Chicago Association bulk large in the development of the evangelist. They were not all spent in dealing with the unconverted, by any means. Sunday's tasks included the securing of speakers for noonday prayer meetings, the conducting of office routine, the raising of money, the distribution of literature, the visiting of saloons and other places to which invitations should be carried, and the following up of persons who had shown an interest in the meetings. Much of it was sanctified drudgery: but it was drill for destiny. The young man saw at close range and with particular detail what sin could do to men; and he also learned the power of the Gospel to make sinners over.

The evangelist often alluded to those days of personal work in Chicago. Such stories as the following have been heard by thousands.

REDEEMING A SON

"I stood on the street one Sunday night giving out tickets inviting men to the men's meeting in Farwell Hall. Along came a young fellow. I should judge he was thirty, who looked prematurely old. He said: 'Pard, will you give me a dime?'

"I said, 'No, sir.'

" 'I want to get somethin' to eat.'

"I said, 'You look to me as though you were a booze-fighter.'

" 'I am.'

" 'I'll not give you money, but I'll get your supper.'

"He said, 'Come on. I haven't eaten for two days.'

" 'My time is not my own until ten o'clock. You go upstairs until then and I'll buy you a good supper and get you a good, warm, clean bed in which to sleep, but I'll not give you the money.'

"He said, 'Thank you, I'll go.' He stayed for the meeting. I saw he was moved, and after the meeting I stood by his side. He wept and I talked to him about Jesus Christ, and he told me this story:

"There were three boys in the family. They lived in Boston. The father died, the will was probated, he was given his portion, took it, started out drinking and gambling. At last he reached Denver, his money was gone, and he got a position as fireman in the Denver and Rio Grande switchyards. His mother kept writing to him, but he told me that he never read the letters. He said that when he saw the postmark and the writing he threw the letter into the firebox, but one day, he couldn't tell why, he opened the letter and it read:

"'Dear———: I haven't heard from you directly, but I am sure that you must need a mother's care in the far-off West, and unless you answer this in a reasonable time I'm going to Denver to see you.' And she went on pleading, as only a mother could, and closed it: 'Your loving mother.'

"He said, 'I threw the letter in the fire and paid no more heed to it. One day about two weeks later I saw a woman coming down the track and I said to the engineer: "That looks like my mother." She drew near, and I said: "Yes, that's Mother." What do you think I did?'

"I said: 'Why you climbed out of your engine, kissed her and asked God to forgive you.'

"He said, 'I did nothing of the kind. I was so low-down, I wouldn't even speak to my mother. She followed me up and down the switchyard and even followed me to my boarding house. I went upstairs, changed my clothes, came down. She said: "Frank, stay and talk with me." I pushed by her and went out and spent the night in sin. I came back in the morning, changed my clothes and went to work. For four days she followed me up and down the switchyards and then she said, "Frank, you have broken my heart, and I am going away to morrow."

"'I happened to be near the depot with the engine when she got on the train and she raised the window and said, "Frank, kiss me good-by." I stood talking with some of my drinking and gambling friends and one man said, "Frank Adsitt, you are a fool to treat your mother like that. Kiss her good-by." I jerked from him and turned back. I heard the conductor call, "All aboard." I heard the bell on the engine ring and the train started out. I heard my mother cry, "Oh, Frank, if you won't kiss me good-by, for God's sake turn and look at me!"

" 'Mr. Sunday, when the train on the Burlington Railroad pulled out of Denver, I stood with my back to my mother. That's nine years ago and I have never seen nor heard from her.'

"I led him to Jesus. I got him a position in the old Exposition building on the lake front. He gave me the money he didn't need for board and washing. I kept his money for months. He came to me one day and asked for it.

"He used to come to the noon meetings every day. Finally I missed him, and I didn't see him again until June, 1893, during the World's Fair he walked into the Y. M. C. A. I said, 'Why, Frank, how do you do?'

"He said, 'How do you know me?'

"I said, 'I have never forgotten you; how is your mother?'

"He smiled, then his face quickly changed to sadness, and he said: 'She is across the street in the Brevoort House. I am taking her to California to fill her last days with sunshine.'

"Three months later, out in Pasadena, she called him to her bedside, drew him down, kissed him, and said, 'Good-by: I can die happy because I know my boy is a Christian.' "

The next class in the university of experience which Sunday entered was that of professional evangelistic work. It was in association with Rev. J. Wilbur Chapman, D.D., well-known Presbyterian evangelist. This invitation came after three years of service in the Chicago Y. M. C. A. Sunday was not yet called to platform speaking as his chief task. Far from it. He was a sort of general handyman for the evangelist. His duties were many. He was advance agent, going ahead to arrange meetings, to organize choirs, to help the local committee of arrangements with its advertising or other preparations, and, in general, tying up loose ends. When tents were used he would help erect them with his own hands. Sunday sold the song books and sermons; helped take up the collection, and, when need arose, spoke from the platform. The persons who wonder at the amazing efficiency for organization displayed by Sunday overlook this apprenticeship to a distinguished evangelist. He was a "practical man" in every aspect of evangelistic campaigns, from organizing a local committee and building the auditorium, to handling and training the converts who came forward.

The providence of all this is clear in retrospect. As for Sunday himself, he was being led by a way that he knew not.

CHAPTER 6

A SHUT DOOR—AND AN
OPEN ONE

*Faith is the beginning of something of which
you can't see the end but in which you believe—*
"BILLY" SUNDAY.

DESTINY'S DOOR turns on small hinges. Almost
everyone can say out of his experience, "If I
had done this, instead of that, the whole course of
my life would have been changed." At many points
in the career of William A. Sunday we see what
small and unrelated incidents determined his future
course in life.

If he had not been sitting on that Chicago curbstone one evening; if the Pacific Garden Mission
workers had failed on that one occasion to go forth,
"Billy" Sunday might have been only one of the
multitude of forgotten baseball players. If he had
not gone to prayer meeting in his new church home
he would not have met the wife who was so largely
a determining factor in his work. If he had not
joined the Y. M. C. A. forces in Chicago he would

not have become Peter Bilhorn's friend and Dr. Chapman's assistant.

Here we come to a very human story; if J. Wilbur Chapman had not suddenly decided to abandon the evangelistic field and return to the pastorate of Bethany Presbyterian Church in Philadelphia, Mr. Sunday would doubtless still be unknown to the world as a great religious leader. This story came from the lips of the evangelist himself. Certain current criticisms of his work were being discussed and he showed himself frankly bewildered, as well as pained, by the hostility displayed toward him on the part of those to whom he looked as leaders and counselors. Off the platform Sunday was one of the most childlike and guileless of men. He grew reminiscent and confidential as he said: "I don't see why they hammer me so. I have just gone on, as the Lord opened the way, trying to do His work. I had no plan for this sort of thing. It is all the Lord's doings. Just look how it all began, and how wonderfully the Lord has cared for me.

"I had given up my Y. M. C. A. work, and was helping Chapman, doing all sorts of jobs: putting up tents, straightening chairs after the meetings and occasionally speaking. Then, during the holidays of 1895-96, I had a telegram from Chapman saying that our work was off. He had decided to return to Bethany Church.

"There I was, out of work, knowing not which way to turn. I had a wife and two children to support. I could not go back to baseball. I had given up my Y. M. C. A. position. I had no money. What should I do? I laid it before the Lord, and in a short while came a telegram from a little town named Garner, Iowa, asking me to come out and conduct meetings. I didn't know anybody out there, and I don't know yet why they asked me to hold meetings. But I went.

"I only had eight sermons, so could not run more than ten days, and that only by taking Saturdays off. That was the beginning of my independent work. From that day to this I have never had to seek a call to do evangelistic work. I have just gone along, entering doors that the Lord has opened one after another. Now I have sermons and invitations for more than two years in advance. I have tried to be true to the Lord and to do just what he wants me to do."

That naïve bit of autobiography reveals the real "Billy" Sunday. He went forward as the doors providentially opened. His career was not one shrewdly planned by himself. Nobody was more surprised at his success than he.

From Garner, Iowa, to Philadelphia, with its most eminent citizens on the committee of arrangements, seems a far cry; but the path was plainly one of Providence. Sunday added to his addresses gleanings from many sources, but he never abated the simplicity of his message. The gospel he preached in his last sermon was that which he heard in the Pacific Garden Rescue Mission so long before.

In childlike faith, this man of straight and unshaded thinking went forward to whatever work offered itself. Nobody knew better than he that it was by no powers of his own that mighty results were achieved: "This is the Lord's doing; it is marvelous in our eyes."

While the Sunday meetings swung a wide orbit they centered in the Middle West. That typically American section of the country was quick to appreciate the evangelist's character and message. He was of them.

When news of the triumphs of this evangelist's unconventionally-phrased gospel began to be carried over the country, the verdict of religious leaders was, " 'Billy' Sunday may do for the Middle West, but the East will not stand him." To the confusion of human wisdom, his most notable work was achieved in the East, in the great cities of Pittsburgh, Scranton, Philadelphia, and Baltimore. An issue of *The American Magazine* carried the results of a voting contest: "Who's the Greatest Man in America." Only one other clergyman (Bishop Vincent of Chautauqua) was mentioned at all, but "Billy" Sunday was tied with Andrew Carnegie and Judge Lindsey for eighth place.

When Sunday visited Washington for a day, his meetings overtopped in public interest the proceedings of the nation's Congress. He was greeted by the President of the United States and many of the leading government officials.

His Philadelphia meetings, January 3 to March 21, 1915, were literally a center of nation-wide attention. No other religious event until then had ever received so much consecutive and contemporaneous newspaper publicity. Pilgrims, clerical and lay, traveled to Philadelphia to attend the services.

The aggregate attendance upon the tabernacle services was more than two million persons. Another million attended the meetings conducted by the eighteen members of the Sunday party, and by the volunteer associates.

The climax of twenty years of arduous campaigning was the Philadelphia experience. The cards signed by trail-hitters numbered 41,724, with churches reporting two and three times as many converts outside of the tabernacle. The last day's recruits numbered 1,858. The farewell gift was

$52,849.97, and the collections for the local expenses were over $50,000. Something more than $15,000 was raised in the meetings for charitable purposes.

CHAPTER 7

CAMPAIGNING FOR CHRIST

Let's quit "fiddling" with religion and do something to bring the world to Christ—"BILLY" SUNDAY.

His AMERICAN BIRTHRIGHT of plain common sense stood Sunday instead of theological training. He was "a practical man," as mechanics say. Kipling's poem on "The American" suits Sunday exactly:

> He turns a keen, untroubled face
> Home to the instant need of things.

So a Sunday evangelistic campaign was a marvel of organization. It spelled efficiency at every turn and is a lesson to the communities which do Christian work in haphazard fashion. Work and faith were written large over every series of Sunday meetings.

Sunday never took a course in psychology, but he understood the crowd-mind. He knew how to deal with multitudes. He saw clearly where the masses must come from, and so he set to work to bring them out of the homes of the workers. He went beyond the church circles and made his appeal to the popular taste. He frankly aimed to strike the average of the common people. He was after that host which too often the preacher knows nothing about.

People had to be set to talking about religion and about the Sunday campaign if the latter was to succeed. Indifference was the foe of all foes to be feared. Even hostile criticism really served a purpose, for it directed attention to the messenger and the message. Knowledge of this was the reason Mr. Sunday always devoted his earliest sermons in a campaign to the subjects likeliest to create comment. These were the discourses that contained the largest proportion of startling views and language.

Part of the task of a man who would move a city for Christ is to consolidate Christian sentiment and create a church consciousness. Sunday was at great pains to get his own "crowd" behind him. He evoked that loyalty which alone makes organized work and war effective.

He insisted that churches must unite before he would visit a city. He asked that they surrender their Sunday services, all uniting in worship in the tabernacle. The campaigns were not "Billy" Sunday meetings: they were an effort toward a revival of religion on the part of the united Christian forces of a community. If anybody thought that the evangelist disparaged the church, he need but recall the particular effort Sunday made to solidify the church folk. He would no more attempt a revival without church co-operation than a general would besiege a city without an army. This Christian unity which he required first of all is a sermon in itself.

Before one looks very deeply into the work of

Evangelist Sunday he must perceive that it was no new message the man spoke, but that it was his modernization of language and of methods that made possible the achieving of great results with the old Gospel.

The preacher of a generation or more ago would have counted it improper to make use of the public press. Sunday depended largely upon the newspapers for spreading his message and promoting interest in the meetings. He did not employ a press agent; he simply extended to the local press all the facilities and co-operation in his power. He was always accessible to reporters and ever ready to assist in their work in any proper way. He made public announcements frequently in his meetings of the cordial assistance he received from the newspapers.

Without expense to anybody and without any scientific experience in this particular field, Sunday demonstrated the power of Christian publicity. The newspapers carried his messages all over the world. The Pittsburgh dailies published special "Sunday Editions." They had thousands of subscribers for the issues containing the evangelist's sermons and many persons have been converted by reading the newspapers. One story tells of a young man in China converted thirteen thousand miles away from the spot where the evangelist was speaking. Sunday made religion "live news." Editors were glad to have copy about him, his work and the campaigns. The uniform experience of the communities he visited was that the Church had had more publicity through his visit than on any other occasion.

After Sunday accepted a city's invitation and a date had been fixed for the meetings, he got the Church people to organize. Before ever a hammer had struck a blow in the building of the Sunday tabernacle, the people had been meeting daily in the homes of the city for concerted prayer for the divine favor upon the campaign.

By the Sunday system of work, every few blocks in the city was made a center for cottage meetings. No politician ever divided a community more carefully than did the Sunday workers. Every section of the city was covered and every block and street. By preference, the meetings were held in the homes of the unconverted. It was a normal experience for conversions to be reported before the evangelist arrived. In Scranton the city was divided into nine districts besides the suburbs. These districts were again subdivided so that one had as many as eighty-four prayer groups. In Pittsburgh between December 2 and 26, 4,137 prayer meetings in private houses were held having a combined attendance of 68,360 persons. These figures were wholly eclipsed by those from Philadelphia.

A stranger in Philadelphia during December, 1914, would have been struck by the number of signs in private homes announcing prayer meetings within. During the entire month these home prayer meetings were held twice a week, averaging more than five thousand meetings on each assigned night, with more than one hundred thousand persons present nightly. This meant an aggregate attendance of nearly a million Christians upon preparatory prayer services!

When tens of thousands of earnest Christians are meeting constantly for united prayer a spirit of expectancy and unity is created which makes sure the success of the revival. Incidentally, there is a welding together of Christian forces that will abide long after the evangelist has gone. These preliminary prayer meetings are a revelation of the tremendous possibilities inherent in the churches of any community. With such prayer buoying him up any preacher could have a revival!

Sunday threw all responsibility on the churches. While he took command of the ship when he arrived, yet he did all in his power to prevent the campaign from being a one-man affair. The local committee must underwrite the expenses; these campaigns were not to be financed by the gifts of the wealthy, but by the rank and file of the church membership accepting responsibility. The guarantees were underwritten in the form of shares and each guarantor received a receipt to be preserved as a memento of the campaign. No guarantor ever had to pay a dollar on his "Billy" Sunday campaign subscription. The evangelist himself raised all of the expense money in the early meetings.

John the Baptist was only a voice; "Billy" Sunday was a voice, plus a bewildering array of committees and assistants and organized machinery. He had committees galore to co-operate in his work—a drilled army of the Lord. In the list of Scranton workers I saw tabulated certain committees, executive, directors, prayer meetings, entertainment, usher, dinner, business-women's, building, nursery, personal workers', decorating, shop-meetings and then a whole list of churches and religious organizations in the city as ex-officio workers!

Wherever he went Sunday erected a special tabernacle for his meetings. There were many reasons for this. The very building of a tabernacle dedicated to this special use helped create an interest in the campaign. Primarily, the evangelist's purposes were practical. In the first place, everything was on the ground floor. Converts cannot easily come forward from a gallery. In addition, existing big buildings rarely had proper acoustics. Most of all Sunday, who had a dread of panics or accidents happening in connection with his meetings, stressed the point that in his tabernacle people had their feet on the ground. The sawdust and tan bark was warm, dustless, sanitary, fireproof and noiseless. "When a crowd gets to walking on a wooden floor," said Sunday—he made a motion of sheer disgust that showed how sensitive he was to any sort of disturbance— "it's the limit."

One of his idiosyncrasies was that he had to have a perfectly still audience. He would stop in the midst of a sermon to let a single person walk down the aisle. When auditors started coughing he stopped preaching. He never let his crowd get out of hand. The result: never so many persons gathered together in one building at one time in such uniform quietness.

The possibilities of panic in a massed multitude of thousands are understood by those who have had to do with crowds. Sunday's watchfulness against this marks the shrewd caution of the man. His tabernacles, no matter whether they seated five, eight, ten, fifteen, or twenty thousand persons, were all built under the direction of his helper, who had traveled with him for years. He knew that nothing would break down, or go askew. His tabernacles were fairly panic-proof. Every aisle, lengthwise and crosswise, ended in a door.

So careful was he of the emergency that might arise for a quick exit that no board in the whole tabernacle fastened with more than two nails. One could put his foot through the side of the wall if there was need. Describing the building of the choir platform Sunday said with a grim shutting of his jaws: "You could run a locomotive over it and never faze it." His own platform, on which he did amazing gymnastic stunts at every meeting, was made to withstand all shocks. About the walls of the tabernacle were fire extinguishers, and a squad of firemen and policemen on duty with every audience.

There was nothing about a Sunday tabernacle to suggest a cathedral. It was a big turtle-back barn of raw, unfinished timber, but it was constructed for its special purpose, and every mechanical device then known was used to assist the speaker's voice. Sunday could make twenty-five thousand persons hear perfectly in one of his tabernacles. A huge sounding board, more useful than beautiful, hung like an inverted sugar scoop over the evangelist's platform.

Behind the platform was the post office, to which the names of converts were sent for the city pastors every day. Here also were the telephones for the use of the press. Adjoining the tabernacle was a nursery for babies, and an emergency hospital with a nurse in attendance. It seemed as if no detail of efficient service has been overlooked by this practical westerner. So well organized was everything that the collection could be taken in an audience of eight thousand persons within three minutes.

This is as good a place as any to raise the point of Mr. Sunday's own compensation. He received a freewill offering made on the last day. The offerings taken in the early weeks were to meet the expenses of the local committee. Mr. Sunday had nothing to do with this. This committee paid approximately half of the expenses of his staff of workers; it also provided a home for the Sunday party during their sojourn. Mr. Sunday himself paid the balance of the expenses of his workers out of the freewill offering which he received on the last day. These gifts reached large figures—over $40,000 in Pittsburgh and $52,849.97 in Philadelphia.

There is a quality in human nature which will

not associate money with religion, and while we hear nobody grumbling at a city's paying thousands of dollars a night for a grand opera performance; yet an evangelist who has ministered to an entire city, lessened the police expense, promoted the general happiness and redeemed hundreds of thousands of lives from open sin to godliness, is accused of mercenariness, because those whom he has served give him an offering as he departs.

Much criticized on the subject of money, Mr. Sunday steadfastly refused to make answer to these strictures or to render an accounting. He insisted that this was entirely a personal matter with him. Nobody who knew him doubted his personal generosity or his sense of stewardship. Intimate friends said that he tithed his income.

Three important departments of the Sunday organization were the choir, the ushers, and the personal-work secretaries. Concerning the first, more will be said in a later chapter. The ushers were by no means ornamental functionaries. They were a drilled regiment, each wth his station of duty and all disciplined to meet any emergency that might arise. In addition to seating the people and taking the collection, they had the difficult task of assisting the officers to keep out the overflow crowds who tried to press into the building that had been filled to its legal capacity. It was quite a normal condition in the Sunday campaigns for thousands of persons to try to crowd their way into the tabernacle after it was full. Sometimes it took football tactics to keep them out.

Without the assistance of the personal-work secretaries the rush forward when the invitation was extended would mean a frantic mob. The recruits were formed into line and directed to the pulpit where they took Mr. Sunday's hand. Then they were guided into the front benches, the name, address and church preference of each secured. While the invitation was being given personal workers all over the building were busy gathering converts.

The tabernacle by no means housed all of the Sunday campaign. There were noon shop meetings, there were noon meetings for business women and luncheon meetings, there were services in the schools, in the jails, in the hospitals, and there were special afternoon parlor meetings where social leaders heard the same message that was given to the men of the street. In a phrase, the entire community was combined by personal activity in order to reach everybody.

The personnel of the Sunday party varied during the years. The first assistant was a soloist and choir leader who continued with the evangelist for eight years. The staff numbered about a dozen workers. Among these helpers, Homer A. Rodeheaver, the chorister; Charles Butler, the soloist; Elijah J. Brown; Fred. R. Seibert, the handy man of the tabernacle; Miss Frances Miller, Miss Grace Saxe, Miss Anna MacLaren, Mrs. Rae Muirehead, Rev. L. K. Peacock, B. D. Ackley, Albert G. Gill, Joseph Speice, the builder, Mrs. and Mr. Asher and Rev. I. E. Honeywell.

CHAPTER 8

"SPEECH—SEASONED WITH SALT"

I want to preach the gospel so plainly that men can come from the factories and not have to bring along a dictionary—"BILLY" SUNDAY.

SUNDAY WAS NOT A SHEPHERD, but a soldier; not a husbandman of a vineyard, but a quarryman. The role he filled more nearly approximates that of the Baptist, or one of the Old Testament prophets, than any other Bible character. The word of the Lord that came to him was not "Comfort ye! comfort ye!" but "Arouse ye! arouse ye!" and "Repent! repent!"

Evangelist Sunday's mission was not conventional, nor may it be judged by conventional standards. He was not a pastor; probably he would have been a failure in the pastorate. Neither would any sensible person expect pastors to resemble "Billy" Sunday; that, too, would have been a calamity.

Here was a man whose clear work it was to attract the attention of the heedless to the claims of the gospel, to awaken a somnolent church, and to call men to repentance. To do this a man must be sensational, just as John the Baptist was sensational —not to mention that Greater One who drew the multitudes by his wonderful works and by his unconventional speech.

When God called this man, he took him straight out of the walks of common life with no other vocabulary than that of ordinary "folks." Americans use words that are alive, new ones being born every hour. "Slang" we call these word pictures, and we bar them from polite speech until the crowbar of custom has jimmied a way for them into the dictionary.

Sunday talked religion as he talked baseball. His words smacked of the street corners, the shop, the athletic field, the crowd of men. Any kind of a fair play that will get the runners to the home plate is good baseball; and any speech that will puncture the shell of human nature's complacency and indifference to religion is good preaching.

Sunday seemed to have recovered some of the prophet's lost art of denunciation. He dared call sin by its proper name. He excoriated the hypocrite. He cared not for feelings of the unfaithful preacher or of the double-living church member. As for the Devil and all his lieutenants, Sunday had for them a sizzling, blistering vocabulary that helped men to loathe sin. His uncompromising attitude is shown by this culled from one of his sermons:

"They say to me, 'Bill, you rub the fur the wrong way.' I don't; let the cats turn 'round."

Again, "Paul said he would rather speak five words that were understood than ten thousand words in an unknown tongue. That hits me. I want people to know what I mean."

Two important points are in Sunday's vigorous

vocabulary: First, that what he said does not sound as bad as it seemed in cold type. Often he was incorrectly reported. The constant contention of his friends was that he should be heard before being criticized. The volume of testimony of all the men who heard him—preachers, professors and purists—was that his addresses which seemed shocking when reported were not shocking when heard.

On the public square in Scranton a great sign was displayed by the local committee:

BE FAIR!
DON'T JUDGE "BILLY" SUNDAY UNTIL YOU
HAVE HEARD HIM YOURSELF.
NO REPORT, VERBAL OR PRINTED, CAN
DO HIM PERFECT JUSTICE.

One Scranton businessman put it this way: "Type is cold; his sermons are hot."

Sunday spoke with his eyes, with his gestures and with every muscle of his body; and all this must be taken into account. Assuredly his message in its totality did not shock anybody. That is why preachers sat through his arraignment of a deficient church and ministry and applauded him. They found in his severest utterances a substantial volume of undoubted truth.

Second, the most vigorous speech was used earliest in an evangelistic campaign. That was one way of stirring up the church, and of attracting attention. Sunday goaded Christians to an interest. Apparently he purposely spoke to arouse resentment, if no other form of interest was awakened in his hearers. The latter part of a Sunday campaign was singularly free from his denunciations, from invective and from slang. There was a clear method in his procedure, which was always followed in about the same order.

Sunday would have been the last man to expect everybody to approve all that he said, either in form or in substance. There remained the unanswerable rejoinder to all criticism of Mr. Sunday's utterances and message: he "delivers the goods." He aroused communities to an interest in religion as no other preacher of his generation. He helped people "get right with God." His campaigns promoted righteousness, diminished wickedness and strengthened the Church.

Some samples of the pungent sort of speech with which Sunday's discourses were flavored:

> Live so that when the final summons comes you will leave something more behind you than an epitaph on a tombstone or an obituary in a newspaper.
>
> You can find anything in the average church today, from a humming bird to a turkey buzzard.
>
> The Lord is not compelled to use theologians. He can take snakes, sticks, or anything else, and use them for the advancement of His cause.
>
> The Lord may have to pile a coffin on your back before he can get you to bend it.
>
> Don't throw your ticket away when the train goes into a tunnel. It will come out on the other side.
>
> The safest pilot is not the fellow that wears the biggest hat, but the man who knows the channels.
>
> If a man goes to Hell he ought to be there, or he wouldn't be there.
>
> I am preaching for the age in which I live. I am just recasting my vocabulary to suit the people of my age instead of Joshua's age.

CHAPTER 9

BATTLING WITH BOOZE

*The man who votes for the saloon is pulling on
the same rope with the devil, whether he knows it
or not*—"BILLY" SUNDAY.

THERE IS A TREMENDOUS military advantage in
having a definite enemy. The sermons that are
aimed at nothing generally hit it. Mr. Sunday was
happiest and most successful when attacking the
liquor evil. Down among the masses of men he
learned for himself the awful malignity of strong
drink. So he fought it. Small wonder the brewers
spent money in attacking him.

There was a ghastly humor in the success the
brewers had in enlisting people to make common
cause with them in discrediting the evangelist.
Shrewd men did come quite generally to the conclusion that they would not give aid and comfort
to the enemies of righteousness whose interests were
best served by criticism of Mr. Sunday. Incidental
questions aside, Sunday did the Lord's work and
was on the Lord's side.

Wherever Sunday went a great temperance awakening followed. In eleven of fifteen Illinois towns where he campaigned "dry" victories were won at the next election. Fifteen hundred saloons were put out of business in a single day in Illinois, largely the result of his work. With characteristic indifference to figures and tabulated results, Sunday kept no record of the communities which went "dry" following his meetings. Up in Pennsylvania's coal regions, with people of widely differing genealogies, many communities went "dry," while individual saloons were starved out. Within about a year of Sunday's visit, the number of saloons was reduced by more than two hundred.

So intense was Sunday's zest for temperance that he would go anywhere possible to deliver a blow against the saloon. He toured Illinois and West Virginia in special trains, campaigning for temperance. During the Sunday campaign in Johnstown ten thousand men in a meeting organized themselves into a "Billy" Sunday Anti-Saloon League. In Iowa literally scores of towns and counties reported as having gone dry as a direct result of the Sunday meetings. Thirteen out of fifteen towns in Illinois visited by Sunday voted out the saloon. West Virginia's temperance leaders utilized Sunday in a whirlwind campaign through the state. He spoke in ten towns in five days, traveling from point to point in a special car. West Virginia went dry by ninety thousand majority. Next to his passion for the conversion of men and women was this consuming antagonism to rum.

More important than his own valiant blows against the saloon was the fact that Sunday made enemies for the liquor business. Practically all of his converts and friends became enthusiastic temperance workers.

Every campaign was full of incidents like that of

the blacksmith, a part of whose business came from a large brewery. When this man became a convert and a temperance "fanatic," as they termed him, the brewers' business was withdrawn. But the loyalty which Sunday infused into his followers, rallied to the man's help, and such a volume of Christian business was turned his way that his conversion and the loss of the brewery trade turned out to his profit.

In the *Outlook* of August 8, 1914, Lewis Edwin Theiss introduced a powerful article: "Industry versus Alcohol," with this "Billy" Sunday story:

"We were discussing 'Billy' Sunday and the economic effect of his work.

" 'The vice-president of the C—— Iron Works told me,' said a manufacturer of railway cars, 'that his company could have afforded to pay its employees a quarter of a million dollars more than their wages during the period that "Billy" Sunday was working among them.'

"The corporation is one of the great steel companies of the country. It employs thousands of men.

" 'Why was that?' I asked.

" 'Because of the increased efficiency of the men. They were steadier. Accidents decreased remarkably. They produced enough extra steel to make their work worth the quarter million additional.'

" 'It is interesting to find that religion has such an effect on everyday life,' I observed.

" 'Religion as such had little to do with it,' replied the carmaker, 'except that it started it. The thing that made those men efficient was cutting out the drink. "Billy" Sunday got them all on the water wagon. They became sober and stayed sober. They could run their machines with steady hands and true eyes. The men themselves realized what a difference it makes. They are strong for prohibition. If the people of Pittsburgh and its vicinity could vote on the temperance question today, the saloons would be wiped out there.'

" 'The manufacturers are strong for prohibition, too. They never gave much thought to the matter before. But this demonstration of "Billy" Sunday's has made us all strong for prohibition. We *know* now that the most of our accidents are due to whisky. For years we have been trying to find a way to secure a high degree of efficiency among our men. We never succeeded. Along comes this preacher and accomplishes more in a few weeks than we have ever been able to do.

" 'We know now that until booze is banished we can never have really efficient workmen. We're fools if we don't profit by what he has shown us. Take it from me, booze has got to go. We are not much interested in the moral side of the matter as such. It is purely a matter of dollars and cents. They say corporations are going to show mighty little soul toward the man who drinks.' "

A great parade of men marked the close of a Sunday campaign. In Scranton the line of march was broken into by a brewer's wagon. The driver was not content with trying to break the line of parade, but he also hurled offensive epithets at Sunday and his converts. Perhaps passive endurance was the virtue called for on this occasion; but it was certainly not the virtue practiced. For those husky mill workers stepped out of line for a moment, bodily overturned the brewer's wagon, and sent the beer kegs rolling in the street, all to the tune of the Sunday war song: "De Brewer's Big Horses Can't Run Over Me."

This song, written by H. S. Taylor, was the most popular in the Sunday campaign. It is by no means a hymn of worship, but rather a battle cry. When thousands of men lifted their voices in this militant refrain, with whistles blowing and bells ringing in the chorus, the effect was fairly thrilling. Words and music were beneath the consideration of the scholarly musician; but they did strike the common mind of the American who wanted a battle hymn.

DE BREWER'S BIG HOSSES.

Oh, de Brewer's big hosses, comin' down de road,
Totin' all around ole Lucifer's load;
Dey step so high, an' dey step so free,
But dem big hosses can't run over me.

CHORUS

Oh, no! boys, oh, no!
De turnpike's free whereber I go,
I'm a temperance ingine, don't you see,
And de Brewer's big hosses can't run over me.

Oh, de licker men's actin' like dey own dis place,
Livin' on de sweat ob de po' man's face,
Dey's fat and sassy as dey can be,
But dem big hosses can't run over me.—CHO.

Oh, I'll harness dem hosses to de temp'rance cart,
Hit 'em wid a gad to gib 'em a start,
I'll teach 'em how far to haw and gee,
For dem big hosses can't run over me.—CHO.

Sunday was the Peter the Hermit of the temperance crusade. He inflammed men's passions for this righteous war. Most critics called his sermon on "booze" his greatest achievement. He treated the theme from all angles—economic, social, human, and religious. When he put a row of boys up on the platform and offered them as one day's contribution to the saloon's grist of manhood which must be maintained, the result was electric; all the militant manhood of the men before him was urged to action. [If you want to read Sunday's famous sermon on "Booze," turn to the Appendix, page 159.

CHAPTER 10

"GIVE ATTENDANCE TO READING"

There are some so-called Christian homes today with books on the shelves of the library that have no more business there than a rattler crawling about on the floor, or poison within the child's reach "BILLY" SUNDAY.

I NEVER HEARD "BILLY" SUNDAY use an ungrammatical sentence," remarked one observer. "He uses a great deal of slang, and many colloquialisms, but not a single error in grammar could I detect. Some of his passages are really beautiful English."

Sunday made diligent effort to supplement his lack of education. He received the equivalent of a high school training in boyhood, which was far more than Lincoln ever had. Nevertheless he had not had the training of the average educated man, much less of a normal minister of the gospel. He was conscious of his limitations: and diligently endeavored to make up for them. When coaching the Northwestern University baseball team in the winter of '87 and '88 he attended classes at the University. He read a great deal and continued his studies. Of course his acquaintance with literature was superficial: but his use of it showed how earnestly he read up on history and literature and the sciences. He made better use of his knowledge of the physical sciences, and of historical allusions, than most men drilled in them. He displayed a proneness for what he himself would call "highbrow stuff," and his disproportionate display of his "book learning" reveals his conscious effort to supply what did not come to him naturally.

Sunday had an eclectic mind. He knew a good thing when he saw it. He was quick to incorporate into his discourses happenings or illustrations wherever found. Moody also was accustomed to do this: he circulated among his friends interleaved Bibles to secure keen comments on Scripture passages. All preachers draw on the storehouses of the past: the old Church Fathers speak every Sunday in the pulpits of Christendom. Nobody originates all that he says. "We are the heirs of all the ages."

At the opening of every one of his campaigns Sunday repeatedly announced that he had drawn his sermon material from wherever he could find it, and that he made no claim to originality. So the qualified critic could detect, in addition to some sermon outlines which were bequests from Dr. Chapman, epigrams from Sam Jones, flashes from Talmage passages from George Stuart, paragraphs from the religious press, apothegms from the great commentators. It was no news to say that Sunday's material was not all original; he avowed this himself. In his gleanings he had help from various associates. Elijah P. Brown's hand could be traced in his sermons: the creator of the "Ram's Horn" proverbs surely was responsible for Sunday's penchant for "throwing stones" at the devil.

Sunday was not an original thinker. He founded no school of scriptural interpretation. He gave no new exposition of Bible passages, nor developed any fresh lines of thought. Nobody heard anything new from him. In every one of his audiences there were probably many persons who had a more scholarly acquaintance with the Bible and with Christian literature.

Temperamentally a conservative, Sunday took the truth taught him by his earliest teachers and adapted and paraphrased and modernized it. In the crucible of his intense personality this truth became "Sundayized." His discourses may have had a variety of origin, but they all sounded like "Billy" Sunday when he delivered them.

A toilsome, painstaking worker, he made elaborate notes of all his sermons, and these he took with him in leather-bound, black books to the platform and followed more or less closely as he spoke. No other man than Sunday could use the rough notes. Often he interjected into one sermon parts of another.

The early copies of Sunday's sermons were taken down more or less correctly in shorthand, and these were reproduced in every city where he went: consequently they lacked the tang and flavor of his later deliveries.

He was alert to glean from all sources. In conversation one morning in Scranton I told him that on the previous day a lawyer friend had characterized a preacher with whom I had been talking by saying, "How much like a preacher he looks, and how little like a man." That afternoon Sunday used this in his sermon and twiddled it under his fingers for a minute or two, paraphrasing it in characteristic Sunday fashion. Doubtless it became part of his permanent stock in trade.

The absolute unconventionality of the man made all this possible. He was not afraid of the most shocking presentation of truth. Thus when speaking at the University of Pennsylvania, he alluded to a professor who had criticized the doctrine of Hell: "That man will not be in Hell five minutes before he knows better." Of course that thrust caught the students. A more discreet and diplomatic person than Sunday would not have dared to say this.

The gospel preached by Sunday was the same that the Church had been teaching for hundreds of years. He knew no modifications. He sat in God's judgment seat in almost every sermon and frequently sent men to Hell by name.

All this may have been deplorable, but it was Sunday. The Bible which he used was an interpreted and annotated edition by one of the most conservative of Bible teachers: this suited Sunday, for he was not of the temperament to be hospitable to new truths that might break forth from the living Word.

This state of mind led him to be extravagant and intolerant in his statements. His hearers were patient with all of this because the body of his teachings was that held by all evangelical Christians. If he had been less cock-sure he would not have been "Billy" Sunday; the great mass of mankind want a religion of authority.

After all, truth is intolerant.

Although lacking technical literary training Sunday was not only a master of living English and of terse, strong, vivid and gripping phrase, but he was also capable of extraordinary flights of eloquence, when he used the chastest and most appropriate language. He has held multitudes spellbound with such passages as these:

GOD'S TOKEN OF LOVE

"Down in Jacksonville, Florida, a man, Judge Owen, quarreled with his betrothed and to try to forget, he went off and worked in a yellow-fever hospital. Finally he caught the disease and had succumbed to it. He had passed the critical stage of the disease, but he was dying. One day his sweetheart met the physician on the street and asked about the judge. 'He's sick,' he told her.

" 'How bad?' she asked.

" ' Well, he's passed the critical stage, but he is dying,' the doctor told her.

" 'But I don't understand,' she said, 'if he's passed the critical stage why isn't he getting well?'

" 'He's dying, of undying love for you, not the fever,' the doctor told her. She asked him to come with her to a florist and he went and there she purchased some smilax and intertwined lilacs and wrote on a card, 'With my love,' and signed her given name.

"The doctor went back to the hospital and his patient was tossing in fitful slumber. He laid the flowers on his breast. He awoke and saw the flowers and buried his head in them. 'Thanks for the flowers, doctor,' he said, but the doctor said, 'They are not from me.'

" 'Then who are they from?'

" 'Guess!'

" 'I can't; tell me.'

" 'I think you'll find the name on the card,' the doctor said, and he looked and read the card, 'With my love.'

" 'Tell me,' he cried, 'did she write that of her free will or did you beg her to do it?' The doctor told him she had begged to do it herself.

"Then you ought to have seen him. The next day

he was sitting up. The next day he ate some gruel.
The next day he was in a chair. The next day he
could hobble on crutches. The next day he threw
one of them away. The next day he threw the cane
away and the next day he could walk pretty well.
On the ninth day there was a quiet wedding in the
annex of the hospital. You laugh; but listen: This
old world is like a hospital. Here are the wards for
the libertines. Here are the wards for the drunkards. Here are the wards for the blasphemers.
Everywhere I look I see scarred humanity.

"Nineteen hundred years ago God looked over
the battlements of Heaven and he picked a basket
of flowers, and then one day he dropped a baby
into the manger at Bethlehem. 'For God so loved
the world, that he gave his only begotten Son, that
whosoever believeth on him should not perish, but
have everlasting life.' What more can He do?

"But God didn't spare Him. They crucified Him,
but He burst the bonds of death and the Holy Spirit
came down. They banished John to the isle of
Patmos and there he wrote the words: 'Behold, I
stand at the door, and knock: if any man hear my
voice, and open the door, I will come in to him, and
sup with him, and he with me.' "

Will you come?

CHAPTER 11

ACROBATIC PREACHING

If nine-tenths of you were as weak physically as you are spiritually, you couldn't walk—"BILLY SUNDAY.

IF "INSPIRATION IS CHIEFLY PERSPIRATION," then there is no doubting the inspiration of Rev. William A. Sunday, D.D. Beyond question he was the most vigorous speaker on the public platform of his day. One editor estimated that he traveled a mile over his platform in every sermon he delivered. There was no other man to compare with him: only an athlete in the pink of condition could endure the grueling exertions to which he subjected himself every day of his campaigns. The stranger who saw him for the first time was certain that he was on the very edge of a complete collapse; but that same remark was made for years.

People understand with their eyes as well as with their ears; and Sunday preached to both. The intensity of his physical exertions certainly enhanced the effect of the preacher's earnestness. No actor on the dramatic stage worked harder. Such passion as dominated Sunday cannot be simulated; it is the soul pouring itself out.

Some of the platform activities of Sunday made spectators gasp. He raced to and fro across the platform. Like a jackknife he fairly doubled up in emphasis. One hand smote the other. His foot stamped the floor as if to destroy it. Once I saw him bring his clenched fist down so hard on the seat of a chair that I feared the blood would flow and the bones be broken. No posture was too extreme for this restless gymnast. Yet it all seemed natural. Like his speech, it was an integral part of the man. Every muscle of his body preached in accord with his voice.

Whenever they are given a chance, most men are prone to break the trammels of sober usage. No layman who went through a "Billy" Sunday campaign had a single word of criticism of the platform gymnastics of the evangelist. Their reasoning was: On the stage, where men undertake to represent a character or a truth, they use all arts and spare themselves not at all. Why should not a man go to greater lengths when dealing with living realities of the utmost importance?

Sunday was a physical sermon. In a unique sense he glorified God with his body. Only a physique kept in tune by clean living and right usage could respond to the terrific and unceasing demands upon it. When in a sermon he alluded to the man who acts no better than a four-footed brute, Sunday was for an instant down on all fours on the platform and you saw that brute. As he pictured a man praying he sank to his knees for a single moment. When he talked of the deathbed penitent as a man waiting to be pumped full of embalming fluid, he could not help going through the motions of pumping in the fluid. He remarked that deathbed repentance was "burning the candle of life in the service of the devil, and then blowing the smoke in God's face." The last phrase was accompanied by "pfouff!" In a dramatic description of the marathon, he pictured the athlete falling prostrate at the goal and—thud! —there lay the evangelist prone on the platform. Only a skilled baseball player, with a long drill in sliding to bases, could fling himself to the floor without serious injury. On many occasions he took off his coat and talked in his shirt sleeves. It seemed impossible for him to stand up behind the pulpit and talk only with his mouth.

The fact is, Sunday was a born actor. He knew how to portray truth by a vocal personality. When he described the traveler playing with a pearl at sea, he tossed an imaginary gem into the air so that the spectators held their breath lest the ship lurch and the jewel lost.

A hint of Sunday's state of mind which drove him to such earnestness and intensity in labor was found in quotations like the following:

"You will agree with me that I'm not a crank; at least I try not to be. I have not preached about my first, second, third or hundredth blessing. I have not talked about baptism or immersion. I told you that while I was here my creed would be: 'With Christ you are saved; without him you are lost.' Are you saved? Are you lost? Going to Heaven? Going to Hell? I have tried to build every sermon right around those questions; and to steer clear of anything else, but I want to say to you in closing, that it is the inspiration of my life, the secret of my earnestness. I never preach a sermon but that I think it may be the last one some fellow will hear or the last I shall ever be privileged to preach. It is an inspiration to me that some day Christ will come.

It may be at morn, when the day is awaking,
When sunlight through darkness and shadow **is**
  breaking,
That Jesus will come in the fullness of glory,
To receive from the world His own.
Oh, joy! Oh, delight! Should we go without dying,
No sickness, no sadness, no sorrow, no crying,
Caught up with the Lord in the clouds of glory
When He comes to receive from the world His
  own.   *   *   *

In dealing with the unreality of many preachers,
Sunday pictured a minister going to the store to buy
groceries for his wife, but using his pulpit manner,
his pulpit tone of voice and his pulpit phraseology.
This was so true to life that it convulsed every congregation that heard it. In these few minutes of
mimicry the evangelist did more to argue for reality
and genuineness and unprofessionalism on the part
of the clergy than could be accomplished by an
hour's lecture.

Another of his famous passages was his portrayal
of the woman nursing a pug dog. You see the woman and you see the dog, and you loved neither one.
Likewise, Sunday mimicked the skinflint hypocrite
in a way to make the man represented loathe himself.

This suggests a second fact about Mr. Sunday's
preaching. He often made people laugh, but rarely
made them cry. His sense of humor was stronger
than his sense of pathos. Now tears and hysterics
are supposed to be part of the stock in trade of the
professional evangelist. No so with Mr. Sunday. He
made sin absurd and foolish as well as wicked; and
he made the sinner ashamed of himself. He recovered for the Church the use of a powerful weapon, the barb of ridicule. There are more instruments of warfare in the gospel armory than the
average preacher commonly uses. Sunday endeav-

ored to employ them all. His favorites seemed to be humor, satire and scorn.

It is a physical performance to preach to crowds of from ten to twenty-five thousand persons every day. Sunday did not have a beautiful voice like many great orators. It was husky and seemed strained and yet it was able to penetrate every corner of the great tabernacles. Nor was he possessed of the oratorical manner, "the grand air" of the rhetorician. Mostly he was direct, informal and colloquial in his utterances.

A very human figure was "Billy" Sunday on the platform. During the preliminaries he enjoyed the music, the responses of the delegations, and any of the informalities that are common accessories of meetings. When he began to speak he was an autocrat and brooked no disturbance. He was less concerned about hurting the feelings of some fidgety, restless usher or auditor than he was about the comfort of the great congregation and its opportunity to hear his message.

Any notion that Sunday loved the limelight is wide of the mark. The fact is he shunned public gaze. It really made him nervous to be pointed out and stared at. That was one reason why he did not go to a hotel, but hired a furnished house for himself and his associates. Here they "camped out" for the period of the campaign, and enjoyed something like the family life of everyday American folk. Their hospitable table put on no more frills than that of the ordinary home. The same cook accompanied the party for months. When a family's religion so commends itself to the cook, it is likely to grade "A No. 1 Hard," like Minnesota wheat.

"Ma," as the whole party called Mrs. Sunday, was responsible for the home, as well as for many meetings. Primarily, though, she looked after "Daddy."

Sunday was the type of man who was quite helpless
with respect to a dozen matters to which a watchful
wife attends. He needed considerable looking after,
and all his friends, from the newspaper men to the
policemen on duty at the house, conspired to take
care of him.

The Pittsburgh authorities assigned a couple of
plain-clothes men to safeguard Sunday. Of course
he "got them" early, as he got most everybody he
came into touch with. These men took care of
Sunday as if he were the famous "millionaire baby"
of Washington and Newport. Not a sense of official
duty, but affectionate personal solicitude animated
those two men who rode in the automobile from
the house to the tabernacle.

Those who came close to the man believed most
in his religion. As one of the newspaper men cov-
ering the meetings said: "The newspaper boys have
all 'hit the trail.' " From Mrs. Sunday, though, it
was learned that there was one bright reporter who
had worked on aspects of the revival who had not
gone forward. He avoided the meetings, and evaded
the personal interviews of the Sunday party. The
evangelist's wife was as solicitous over that one
young man's spiritual welfare as if he had been
one of her own four children.

Ten of the policemen stationed at the tabernacle
went forward one night in Pittsburgh. Twenty
others were waiting to "hit the trail" in a group,
taking their families with them, it was reported.

The personal side of Mr. Sunday was wholesome
_nd satisfactory. He was a simple, modest chap,
marked by the ways of the Middle West.

CHAPTER 12

"THE OLD-TIME RELIGION"

I am an old-fashioned preacher of the old-time religion, that has warmed this cold world's heart for two thousand years—"BILLY" SUNDAY.

MODERN TO THE LAST MINUTE Sunday's methods may have been, but his message was unmistakably the "old-time religion." He believed his beliefs without a question. There was no twilight zone in his intellectual processes; no mental reservation in his preaching. He was sure that man was lost without Christ, that only by the acceptance of the Saviour can fallen humanity find salvation. He was as sure of Hell as of Heaven, and for all modernized varieties of religion he had only scorn.

In no single particular was Mr. Sunday's work more valuable than in its revelation of the power of positive conviction to attract and convert multitudes. The world wants faith. "Intolerant," cry the scholars of Sunday; but the hungry myriads accepted him as their spiritual guide to peace, and joy, and righteousness. The world wants a religion with salvation in it; speculation does not interest the average man who seeks deliverance from sin in himself and in the world. He does not hope to be evoluted into holiness; he wants to be redeemed.

"Modernists" sputtered and fumed and railed at Sunday and his work: but they could not deny that he led men and women into new lives of holiness, happiness and helpfulness. Churches were enlarged and righteousness promoted by the old, blood-stained way of the cross. The revivals which followed the preaching of Evangelist Sunday are supplemented to the Book of the Acts. His theology is summed up in the words Peter used in referring to Jesus: "There is none other name under heaven given among men whereby we must be saved."

One of Sunday's favorite sayings was: "I don't know any more about theology than a jack rabbit does about ping-pong, but I'm on my way to glory." That really did not fully express the evangelist's point. He was arguing that "theology bears the same relation to Christianity that botany does to flowers, or astronomy to the stars. Botany is rewritten, but the flowers remain the same. Theology changes (I have no objection to your new theology when it tries to make the truths of Christianity clearer), but Christianity abides. Nobody is kept out of Heaven because he does not understand theology. It is not theology that saves, but Christ; it is not the sawdust trail that saves, but Christ in the motive that makes you hit the trail.

"I believe the Bible is the Word of God from cover to cover. I believe that the man who magnifies the Word of God in his preaching is the man whom God will honor. Why do such names stand out on the pages of history as Wesley, Whitefield, Finney and Martin Luther Because of their fearless denunciation of all sin, and because they preach Jesus Christ without fear or favor.

"But somebody says a revival is abnormal. You lie! Do you mean to tell me that the godless, card-playing conditions of the church are normal? I say they are not, but it is the abnormal state. It is the sin-eaten, apathetic condition of the church that is abnormal. It is the 'Dutch lunch' and beer party, card parties and the like, that are abnormal. I say that they lie when they say that a revival is an abnormal condition in the church.

"What we need is the old-time kind of revival that will cause you to love your neighbors, and quit talking about them. A revival that will make you pay your debts, and have family prayers. Get that kind and then you will see that a revival means a very different condition from what people believe it does.

"Christianity means a lot more than church membership. Many an old skinflint is not fit for the balm of Gilead until you give him a fly blister and get after him with a currycomb. There are too many Sunday school teachers who are godless card-players, beer, wine and champagne drinkers. No wonder the kids are going to the devil. No wonder your children grow up like cattle when you have no form of prayer in the home." [For a sample gospel sermon by Sunday, see the Appendix, page 000.]

CHAPTER 13

"HITTING THE SAWDUST TRAIL"

Come and accept my Christ—"BILLY" SUNDAY.

OUT IN THE PUGET SOUND COUNTRY, where the sawdust aisles and the rough tabernacle made an especial appeal to the woodsmen, the phrase, "Hitting the sawdust trail" came into use in Mr. Sunday's meetings. The figure was luminous. For was not this the trail that led the lost to salvation, the way Home to the Father's house?

The metaphor appealed to the American public, which relishes all that savors of our people's most primitive life. Besides, the novel designation serves well the taste of a nation which is singularly reticent concerning its finer feelings, and delights to cloak its loftiest sentiments beneath slang phrases. The person who rails at "hitting the trail" as an irreverent phrase has something to learn. Tens of thousands of persons have enshrined the homely phrase in the sanctuary of their deepest spiritual experience.

The scene itself, when Mr. Sunday called for converts to come forward and take his hand, in token of the purpose to accept and follow Christ was beyond words. Human speech cannot do justice to the picture for good reason. This is one of those crises in human life the portrayal of which makes the highest form of literature. A Victor Hugo could find a dozen novels in each night's experience in the "Billy" Sunday Tabernacle.

This was an hour of bared souls. The great transaction between man and his Maker was under way. The streams of life were changing their course. Character and destiny were being altered. The old Roman "Sacramentum," when the soldiers gave allegiance with uplifted hand, crying, "This for me! This for me!" could not have been more impressive than one of those great outpourings of human life up the sawdust aisle to the front to grasp the preacher's hand, in declaration that henceforth their all would be dedicated to the Christ of Calvary.

The greatness of the scene was at first incomprehensible. There were no parallels for it in all the history of Protestantism until that time. An unschooled American commoner, who could not pass the entrance examinations of any theological seminary in the land, publicly grasped the hands of approximately a quarter of a million persons, who by that token said, in the presence of the great congregation, that they thereby vowed allegiance to their Saviour and Lord. Moody, Whitefield, Finney, did not leave such a record of converts.

A dramatic imagination is needed to perceive even a fragment of what is meant by such an army of Christian recruits. The magnitude of the host was scarcely revealed by the statement that these converts more than equaled the number of inhabitants of the states of Delaware or Arizona of that day.

It far surpassed those of Nevada and Wyoming. Imagine a state made up wholly of zealous disciples of Christ! Of the one hundred largest cities in the United States there were only nineteen with more inhabitants than the total number of persons who "hit the trail" at the Sunday meetings.

Break up that vast host into its component parts. Each was an individual whose experience was as real and distinctive as if there never had been another human soul to come face to face with God. To one the act meant a clean break with a life of open sin. To another it implied a restored home and a return to respectability. To a young person it signified entrance upon a life of Christian service; to that one a separation from all old associations. Some gave up unworthy callings. Others healed old feuds and made restitution for ancient wrongs. One young woman in accepting Christ knew that she must reject the man she had meant to marry. To many men it implied a severance of old political relations. Far and wide and deep that sawdust trail ran; and the record is written in the sweat of agonizing souls.

The consequences of conversion stagger the imagination: this process is still the greatest social force of the age.

Little wonder that persons of discernment journeyed long distances to attend a Sunday meeting, and to witness this appeal for converts to "hit the trail." This is vital religion. If a wedding casts its dramatic spell upon the imagination; if a political election stirs the sluggish deeps of the popular mind; if a battle calls for newspaper "extras"; if an execution arrests popular attention by its element of the mystery of life becoming death—then, by so much and more, that critical, decisive moment in the lives of living men and women gripped the mind by its intense human interest. What issues, for time and eternity, were being determined by the step! The great romance was enacted daily at the Sunday meetings.

These converts were intent upon the most sacred experience that ever comes to mortal. Through what soul struggles they passed, what renunciations they made, what futures they faced, only God and Heaven's hosts know! The crowd dimly sensed all this. There was an instinctive appreciation of the dramatic in the multitude. So the evangelist's appeal was followed by an added tenseness, a straining of necks, a general rising to behold the expected procession.

A more simple and unecclesiastical setting for this tremendous scene could scarcely be devised. The plain board platform, about six feet high, and fifteen feet long, was covered by a carpet. Its only furniture was a secondhand walnut pulpit, directly under the huge sounding board; and one plain wooden chair, "a kitchen chair," a housewife would call it. Then the invitation was given for all who wanted to come out on the side of Christ to come forward and grasp Sunday's hand.

From all parts of the great building they pressed forward. A step before the eyes of friends, neighbors, work-fellows. It called for courage, for this was a life enlistment. Young men crowded toward the platform, where the helpers formed them into a swiftly moving line,—dozens and scores of boys and men in the first flush of manhood. Occasionally an old person was in the line; oftener it was a boy or girl, a mother with her son.

How differently the converts acted. Some had streaming eyes. Others wore faces radiant with the light of a new hope. Still others had the tense, set features of gladiators entering the arena. For min-

ute after minute the procession continued. When
a well-known person went forward, the crowd
cheered. . . .

The first to take the evangelist's hand was a
young Negro boy. The girl who followed might be
a stenographer. Young men were a large part of
the recruits; a dozen fine-looking members of an
athletic club in a body while the crowd cheered;
evidently somebody had been doing personal work
there.

Contrasts were too common to mention. A delicate lady's kid-gloved hand reached up to that of the
evangelist; the next the grimy, calloused hand of a
blue-shirted miner. Was the world to find a new
moral or religious leader in the person of some one
of those bright-faced youths who made this sign of
dedication?

An old man, with a strong face would come; evidently a personality of force. Twice the evangelist
patted the head bowed before him, in pleasure over
the aged recruit. He seemed reluctant to let the
old man go; but the children crowded behind him;
no convert could have more than a handclasp and
a word.

Around the platform the crowd resembled a hive
of bees just before swarming. Stir, motion, anima-
tion seemed to create a scene of confusion. But
there was order and purpose in it all. The occu-
pants of the front seats were moved out to make
way for the converts, there to be talked with, and to
sign cards that were turned over to the local pastors.

Personal workers got into action. The ministers
streamed down! The Young Men's Christian Association secretary, and the Salvation Army soldiers,
and the members of the choir, wearing Christian
Endeavor and Bible class badges! This was religion
in action.

Homer Rodeheaver, the chorister, leaned upon the piano and softly led the great choir in "Almost Persuaded." The musical invitation continued while the work went on in front. It was undisturbed by an occasional appeal from the evangelist. The song quickly changed to "Oh, Where Is My Wandering Boy Tonight?" and then, as the volume of penitents increased, "I Am Coming Home" and "Ring the Bells of Heaven, There Is Joy Today!" All this was psychological; it fostered the mood which the sermon created. Music mellowed as many hearts as spoken words.

All the while Sunday was shaking hands. At first he leaned far over, for the platform was more than six feet high. Sometimes it seemed as if he would lose his balance. To reach down he stood on his left foot, with his right leg extended straight behind him, the foot higher than his head. No one posture was retained long. Often he dipped down with a swinging circular motion, like a pitcher about to throw a ball. Never was man more lavish of his vital energy! Work such as this makes terrific draughts on a man's nerve force.

As the converts increased, he lifted a trapdoor in the platform, which permitted him to stand three feet nearer the people. Still they came, often each led by some personal worker. A Scandinavian was led forward in one meeting; ten minutes later he brought his wife.

A collarless, ragged, weak-faced slave of dissipation came next to a beautiful girl in the dew of her youth. An old, white-haired Negro, leaning on a staff, came forward, then a little child. Veritably all sorts and conditions of people came.

In a particular session, a big delegation of railroad men were present. The evangelist kept turning to them, with an occasional "Come on, Erie!"

Memories of his own days as a railroad brakeman evidently worked within him, and he seized a green lantern and waved it. "A clear track ahead!" Toward those men he was most urgent, beckoning with a white railroad flag which he had taken from the decorations. When the master mechanic "hit the trail" there was cheering from the crowd. Sunday himself showed a delight that was exhibited over none of the society folk who came.

Rare and remarkable as were these scenes in religious history, they came nightly in the Sunday tabernacle. Two hundred, three hundred, five hundred, one thousand converts were common.

Chapter 14

THE SERVICE OF SOCIETY

A lot of people think a man needs a new grand-father, sanitation, and a new shirt, when what he needs is a new heart—"BILLY" SUNDAY.

SOME DAY a learned university professor, with a string of titles after his name, will startle the world by breaking away from the present conventionalism in sociology, and will conduct elaborate laboratory experiments in human betterment. His conclusion will surely be that the most potent force for the service of society—the shortest, surest way of bettering the human race—is by the fresh, clear, sincere and insistent preaching of the Gospel of Jesus Christ.

Of course, the New Testament has been teaching that for many centuries, but the world has not yet comprehended the practicability of the program. Your learned professor may prove, by literally thousands of incidents, that honesty, chastity, brotherliness, and idealism have been more definitely promoted by revivals of religion than by legislative or education programs. All that the social reformers desire may be most quickly secured by straight preaching of the Gospel. The short cut to a better social order is by way of converted men and women.

If there is one phrase which, better than another, would describe "Billy" Sunday campaigns it is "restitution and righteousness." In season and out, the evangelist insisted upon a changed life as the first consequence of conversion. His message ran on this wise:

"You ought to live so that every one who comes near you will know that you are a Christian. Do you? Does your milkman know that you are a Christian? Does the man who brings your laundry know that you belong to church? Does the man who hauls away your ashes know that you are a Christian? Does your newsboy know that you have religion? Does the butcher know that you are on your way to Heaven?

"If you had to get into Heaven on the testimony of your washerwoman, could you make it? If your getting into Heaven depended on what your dressmaker knows about your religion, would you land? If your husband had to gain admittance to Heaven on the testimony of his stenographer, could he do it? If his salvation depended on what his clerks tell about him, would he get there? A man ought to be as religious in business as he is in church. He ought to be as religious in buying and selling as he is in praying."

Here is how the Philadelphia *North American,* characterized the ethical and political effectiveness of Mr. Sunday:

"Billy" Sunday, derided by many as a sensational evangelist, has created a political revolution in Allegheny County. What years of reform work could not do he has wrought in a few short weeks. Old line "practical" politicians, the men who did the dirty work for the political gang, are now zealous for temperance, righteousness and religion.

Judges on the bench, grand dames of society, millionaire businessmen, in common with the great host of undistinguished men and women in homes, mills, offices, and shops, have been fired by this amazing prophet with burning zeal for practical religion.

An unexpected, unpredicted and unprecedented social force has been unleashed. Not to reckon with this is to be blind to the phase of Sunday's work which bulks larger than his picturesque vocabulary or his acrobatic earnestness.

In the presence of this man's work all attempts to classify religious activities as either "evangelistic" or "social service" fell into confusion.

Sunday could have claimed for himself that he was an evangelist, and an evangelist only. He repudiated a Christian program that was merely palliative or ameliorative. To his thinking the church had more fundamental business than running soup kitchens or gymnasiums or oyster suppers. All his peerless powers of ridicule were frequently turned upon the frail and lonely oyster in the tureen of a money-making church supper.

Nevertheless, the results of Sunday's preaching were primarily social and ethical. He was a veritable besom of righteousness sweeping through a community. The wife who neglects her cooking, mending and home-making; the employer who does not deal squarely with his workers; the rich man who rents his property for low purposes or is tied up in crooked business in any wise; the workman who is not on "his job"; the gossip and the slanderer; the idle creatures of fashion; the Christian who is not a good person to live with, the selfish, the sour, the unbrotherly—all such found themselves under the devastating harrow of this flaming preacher's biting, burning, excoriating condemnation. "A scourge for morality" was the way one minister described him; he was, and far more.

After the whole field of philanthropy and reform have been traversed it still remains true that the fundamental reform of all is the cleaning up of the lives and the lifting up of the ideals of the people. That is indisputably what Sunday did. He sweetened life and promoted a wholesome, friendly, helpful and cheerful state of mind on the part of those whom he influenced.

Assuredly it is basic betterment to cause men to quit their drunkenness and lechery and profanity. All the white-slave or social-evil commissions that have ever met have done less to put a passion for purity into the minds of men and women than this one man's preaching has done. The safest communities in the country for young men and young women were those which had gone through a "Billy" Sunday revival.

One cannot cease to exult at the fashion in which the evangelist made the Gospel synonymous with clean living. All the considerations that weighed to lead persons to go forward to grasp the evangelist's hand, also operated to make them partisans of purity and probity.

Put into three terse phrases, Sunday's whole message was: "Quit your meanness. Confess Christ. Get busy for Him among men." There were no finely spun spiritual sophistries in Sunday's preaching. He sometimes spoke quite rudely of that conception of a "higher spiritual life" which draws Christians apart from the world in a self-complacent consciousness of superiority.

His was not a mystical, meditative faith. It was dynamic, practical, immediate. According to his ever-recurring reasoning, if one was not passing on the fruits of religion to somebody else—if one was not hitting hard blows at the devil or really doing definite tasks for God and the other man—then one had not the real brand of Christianity. Sunday's preaching had hands, with "punch" to them, as well as lift; and feet, with "kick" in them, as well as ministry.

Like a colliery mined on many levels, Sunday's preaching reached all classes. Everybody can appreciate the social service value of converting a gutter loafer and making him a self-supporting workman. Is it any less social service to convert a man—I shall cite an actual instance from Pittsburgh—who had lost a twelve-thousand-dollar-a-year position through dissipation, and so thoroughly to help him find himself that before the meetings were over he was back in his old office, once more drawing one thousand dollars a month?

To a student of the campaigns, it seems as if business sensed, better than the preachers, the economic waste of sin.

A careful and discriminating thinker, the Rev. Joseph H. Odell, D.D., formerly pastor of the Second Presbyterian Church of Scranton, wrote an estimate of "Billy" Sunday and his work for *The Outlook,* in which he explained why his church which had been opposed to the coming of the evangelist, reversed its vote:

Testimony, direct and cumulative, reached the ears of the same refined and reverent men and women. The young businessmen, even those from the great universities, paused to consider. The testimony that changed the attitudes of the church came from judges, lawyers, heads of corporations and well-known society leaders in their respective communities. The testimony was phenomenally concurrent in this: that, while it did not endorse the revivalist's methods, or accept his theological system, or condone his roughness and rudeness, it proved that the preaching produced results.

"Produced results!" Every one understood the phrase; in the business world it is talismanic. As the result of the "Billy" Sunday campaigns—anywhere and everywhere—drunkards became sober, thieves became honest, multitudes of people engaged themselves in the study of the Bible, thousands confessed their faith in Jesus Christ as the Saviour of the world, and all the quiescent righteousness of the community grew brave and belligerent against vice, intemperance, gambling, and political dishonesty.

During the last week of February I went to Pittsburgh for the purpose of eliciting interest in the candidacy of J. Benjamin Dimmick for the nomination of United States Senator. "Billy" Sunday had closed his Pittsburgh campaign a few days earlier. My task was easy. A group of practical politicians met Mr. Dimmick at dinner. They were the men who had worked the wards of Allegheny County on behalf of Penrose and the liquor interests for years. Together they were worth many thousands of votes to any candidate; in fact, they were the political balance of power in that county. They knew everything that men could know about the ballot, and some things that no man should know. Solidly, resolutely, and passionately they repudiated Penrose. "No one can get our endorsement in Allegheny County, even for the office of dog-catcher, who is not anti-booze and anti-Penrose," they asserted. When asked the secret of their crusader-like zeal against the alliance of liquor and politics, they frankly ascribed it to "Billy" Sunday; they had been born again—no idle phrase with them—in the vast whale-back tabernacle under the preaching of the baseball evangelist.

Sunday dealt with the very springs of action; he sought to help men get right back to the furthermost motives of the mind. "If you're born again, you won't live knowingly in sin. This does not mean that a Christian cannot sin, but that he does

not want to sin." This truth the evangelist illustrated by the difference between a hog and a sheep.
The sheep may fall into the mud, but it hates it
and scrambles out. A hog loves the mud and wal-
lows in it.

Nobody can measure the results of the social
forces which this simple-thinking evangelist set to
work. His figure of the dwarf who could switch on
the electric lights in a room as easily as a giant,
comes to mind. He has sent into Christian work
men who can do a kind of service impossible to Sunday himself. Thus, one of Sunday's converts in
Wichita was Henry J. Allen, editor of *The Beacon*,
Progressive candidate for governor. Mr. Allen became a member of one of the celebrated "Gospel
Teams," which after the Sunday meetings, toured
Kansas and neighboring states. It was in a meeting
held by this band that William Allen White, the
famous editor, author and publisher, took a definite
stand for Christ and Christian work. One of the
most interesting facts about Sunday's work was that
the three greatest editors in the State of Kansas of
that day became direct or indirect converts. An
"endless chain" letter would be easier to overtake
than the effects of a Sunday revival campaign.

In the face of the mass of testimony of this sort
is it any wonder that businessmen deemed a Sunday
campaign worth all it cost, merely as an ethical
movement? The quickest and cheapest way to im-
prove morals and the morale of a city is by a revival. Thus it was illuminating to learn that there
were 650 fewer inmates in the Allegheny County
jail, during the period of the Sunday revival meetings, than during the same time in the preceding
year.

From Pittsburgh came the remarkable story that
the Cambria Steel Company established a religious

department in connection with its plant, and placed a regularly ordained minister in charge of it. This as an avowed result of the Sunday campaign.

The Rev. Dr. Maitland Alexander, D.D., pastor of the First Presbyterian Church of Pittsburgh, said:

> "Billy" Sunday succeeded in moving the city of Pittsburgh from one end to the other. That, to my mind, was the greatest result of the meetings. It was easy to talk about religion in Pittsburgh. Men especially thought of it as never before, and the great majority were no longer in the middle of the road. They were on one side or the other. No man could speak to men with such telling effect as "Billy" Sunday.
>
> It was necessary in my own church, which when packed, holds 3200 persons, to hold special meetings for different groups, such as lawyers, doctors and bankers. They were always crowded. In the big tabernacle, which was built for the campaign and holds more than 20,000 persons, the men from the big steel shops, after the second week, came in groups of from one to three thousand, in many cases headed by their leading officers.

Dr. Alexander said that the Sunday campaign had added 419 members to his church.

One of the striking consequences of the Sunday campaign in Scranton was the development of the "Garage Bible Class." This was originally a Wilkes-Barre poker club. As the story was told by Mr. Thos. H. Atherton, a Wilkes-Barre attorney, the Garage Bible Class was originally a group of wealthy men meeting at different homes every week for a poker game. One man bet a friend fifteen dollars that he would not go to hear "Billy" Sunday. One by one, however, the men found themselves unable to resist the lure of the tabernacle. As a result the poker club was abandoned. In a garage belonging to one of the men they organized a Bible class. They adopted a rule that no Christian should be added to their ranks. They made Christians out of the unconverted.

From this one gets some conception of the tug and pull of the Sunday tabernacle. The temptation to attend became well nigh irresistible. All the streams of the community life flowed toward the great edifice where the baseball evangelist enunciated his simple message. A writer in *The Churchman* said:

This evangelist made religion a subject of ordinary conversation. People talked about their souls as freely as about their breakfast. He went into the homes of the rich, dropped his wildness of speech, and made society women cry with shame and contrition. One's eternal welfare became the topic of the dinner table, not only in the slums but in the houses of fashion. It sounds incredible, and it is not a fact to be grasped by the mere reading of it, but the citizens of Pittsburgh forgot to be ashamed to mention prayer and forgiveness of sin; the name of Christ began to be used with simpleness and readiness and reverence by men who, two months before, employed it only as a by-word. City politicians came forward and asked for prayer. The daily newspapers gave more space to salvation than they did to scandal, not for one day, but for day after day and week after week. As a mere spectacle of a whole modern city enthralled by the Gospel it was astonishing, unbelievable, unprecedented.

Because he preached both to employers and to employed, Sunday was able to apply the healing salt of the Gospel at the point of contact between the two. From Columbus it was reported that a number of businessmen voluntarily increased the wages of their helpers, especially the women, because of the evangelist's utterances.

A horse jockey out West reached the core of the matter when he said concerning "Billy" Sunday, "He sets people to thinking about other people."

There you have the genesis and genius and goal of
social service. No other force that operates among
men is equal to the inspiration and inhibitions of
Christianity in the minds of individuals. The greatest service that can be done to any community is to
set a considerable proportion of its people to en-
deavoring honestly to live out the ideals of Jesus
Christ.

It is simply impossible to enumerate anything like
a representative number of incidents of the community value of Sunday's work. They come from
every angle and in the most unexpected ways. A
banker, not a member of any church, received a
letter from a man who had defrauded him out of a
small sum of money years before. The banker had
never known anything about the matter and did not
recall the man's name. What did amaze him, and
set him to showing the letter to all his friends, was
this man's restitution, accompanied by a testimony
to his new discipleship to Jesus Christ, upon which
he had entered at the invitation of "Billy" Sunday.

The imagination is stirred by a contemplation of
what these individual cases of regeneration imply.
Consider the homes reunited; consider the happy
firesides that once were the scene of misery; measure, if you can, the new joy that came to tens of
thousands of lives in the knowledge that they gave
themselves unreservedly to the service of Jesus
Christ.

The dramatic, human side of it strikes one. A
young man "hit the trail" at Scranton. The young
man was the only son of his parents and the hope
of two converging family lines. Grandparents and
parents, uncles and aunts, pinned all of their ex-
pectations on this young man. He was a youth of
parts and of force and a personality in the community. On the night when he came up the "saw-

dust trail" to grasp the evangelist's hand, his aged grandfather and his mother wept tears of joy. The grandfather himself "hit the trail" at the Scranton meetings and spent his time afterward largely in Christian work. It is impossible to say how this young man's future might have spelled sorrow or joy for the family circle that had concentrated their hopes on him. His conversion brought to them a boon such as money could not have bought nor kings conferred.

There was a cultivated, middle-aged German, a well-known citizen, who was an avowed atheist. He openly scoffed at religion. He was unable, however, to resist the allurement of the Sunday meetings, and he went with his wife one night merely to "see the show." That one sermon broke down the philosophy of years, and the atheist and his wife became converts. His three sons followed suit, so that the family of five adults were led into the Christian life by this evangelist untaught of the schools. One of the sons became a member of the State Y. M. C. A. Committee.

A western businessman, who is interested in the Young Men's Christian Association, reported that one cold, rainy winter's day he happened into the Association Building in Youngstown, Ohio. He found a crowd of men streaming into a meeting, and because the day was so unpropitious, he asked the character of the gathering. He was told that it was the regular meeting of the Christian Workers' Band, gathered to report on the week's activities. The men had been converted to Christ and Christian work, by "Billy" Sunday, and their meeting had continued, although a year had passed since the evangelist's presence in Youngstown. Said the friend, "That room was crowded. One after another the men got up and told what definite Christian work they had been doing in the previous seven days. They had been holding meetings in all sorts of places, and had been doing a variety of personal work besides, so that there were a number of converts to be reported at the meeting I attended." To have set that force in operation so that it would continue to work with undiminished zeal after twelve months of routine existence, was a greater achievement than to preach a "Billy" Sunday sermon.

There is a sufficient body of evidence to show that the work of "Billy" Sunday did not end when the evangelist left the community. The crowd spirit had been called forth to the service of the Master. Young people and old were given a new and overmastering interest in life. They had something definite to do for the world and a definite group with which to ally themselves.

One result was a tremendous growth of Bible classes for men and women and a manifestation of the crusader spirit which made itself felt in cleaned-up communities and in overthrown corruption in politics. So far as the Sunday campaigns may be said to have had a badge, it was the little red and white bull's-eye pin of the Organized Adult Bible Classes.

Six months after the Scranton campaign five thousand persons attended a "Trail Hitters'" picnic, where the day's events were scheduled under two headings, "athletic" and "prayer." When wholesome recreation comes thus to be permeated with the spirit of devotion something like an ideal state of society has come to pass for at least one group of people.

In more ways than the one meant by his critics, Sunday's work was sensational. What could be more striking than the visit on Sunday, October 25, 1914, of approximately a thousand converts from Scranton to the churches of Philadelphia, to help prepare them for their approaching Sunday campaign? Special trains were necessary to bring this great detachment of men the distance of three hundred miles. They went in bands of four, being distributed among the churches of the city, to hold morning and evening services, and in the afternoon conducting neighborhood mass meetings. These men were by no means all trained speakers, but they were witnesses; their testimony could scarcely fail to produce a powerful influence upon the city. That, on a large scale, was what Sunday converts were doing in a multitude of places.

The truth stands out that "Billy" Sunday set a host of people to thinking that this world's problems are to be solved, and its betterment secured, not by any new-fangled methods, but along the old and tested line of transforming individual characters through the redeeming power of the crucified Son of God. Salvation is surest social service.

The evangelist's sermons were filled with the life stories of the men and women. The following is only one of many:

"I was at one time in a town in Nebraska and the people kept telling me about one man. 'There is one man here, if you can get him he is good for one hundred men for Christ.' I said: 'Who is he?'

" 'John Champenoy. He is the miller.' I said to Mr. Preston, who was then a minister: 'Have you been to see him?' 'No.' I asked another minister if he had been to see the fellow and he said no. I asked the United Presbyterian preacher (they have a college out there), and he said no, he hadn't been around to see him.

"I said: 'Well, I guess I'll go around to see him. I found the fellow seated in a chair teetered back against the wall smoking. I said: 'Is this Mr. Champenoy?' 'Yes, sir, that's my name.' He got up and took me by the hand. I said: 'My name is Sunday; I'm down at the church preaching. A good many have been talking to me about you and I came down to see you and ask you to give your heart to God.' He looked at me, walked to the cupboard, opened the door, took out a half-pint flask of whisky and threw it out on a pile of stones.

"He then turned around, took me by the hand, and as the tears rolled down his cheeks he said: 'I have lived in this town nineteen years and you are the first man that has ever asked me to be a Christian.'

"He said: 'They point their finger at me and call me an old drunkard. They don't want my wife around with their wives because her husband is a drunkard. Their children won't play with our babies. They go by my house to Sunday school and church, but they never ask us to go. They pass us by. I never go near the church. I am a member of the lodge. I am a Mason and I went to the church eleven years ago when a member of the lodge died, but I've never been back and I said I never would go.'

"I said: 'You don't want to treat the church that way. God isn't to blame, is He?'

" 'No.'

" 'The church isn't to blame, is it?'

" 'No.'

" 'Christ isn't to blame?'

" 'No.'

" 'You wouldn't think much of me if I would walk up and slap your wife because you kept a dog I didn't like, would you? Then don't slap God in the face because there are some hypocrites in the church that you don't like and who are treating you badly. God is all right. He never treated you badly. Come up and hear me preach, will you, John?'

" 'Yes, I'll come tonight.'

"I said: 'All right, the Lord bless you and I will pray for you.' He came; the seats were all filled and they crowded him down the side aisle. I can see him now standing there, with his hat in his hand, leaning against the wall looking at me. He never took his eyes off me. When I got through and gave the invitation he never waited for them to let him out. He walked over the backs of the seats, took his stand for Jesus Christ, and in less than a week seventy-eight men followed him into the kingdom of God. They elected that man chairman of the civic federation and he cleaned the town up for Jesus Christ and led the hosts of righteousness from then on. Men do care to talk about Jesus Christ and about their souls. 'No man cares for my soul.' That's what's the trouble. They are anxious and waiting for some one to come."

CHAPTER 15

GIVING THE DEVIL HIS DUE

I know there is a devil for two reasons; first, the Bible declares it; and second, I have done business with him—"BILLY" SUNDAY.

THE PRINCE OF DARKNESS was no more real to Martin Luther, when he flung his ink-well at the devil, than he was to "Billy" Sunday. He seemed never long out of the evangelist's thought. Sunday regarded him as his most personal and individual foe. Scarcely a day passed that he did not direct his attention publicly to the devil. He addressed him and defied him, and he cited Satan as a sufficient explanation for most of the world's afflictions.

There are many delicate shadings and degrees and differentiations in theology—but Sunday did not know them. He never spoke in semitones, nor thought in a nebulous way. His mind and his word were at one with his baseball skill—a swift, straight passage between two points. With him men were either sheep or goats; there were no hybrids. Their destination was Heaven or Hell, and their master, God or the devil.

He believed in the devil firmly, picturesquely; and fought him without fear. His characterizations of the devil were hair-raising. It is far easier for the average man, close down to the ruck and red realities of life, to believe in the devil, whose work he well knows, than it is for the cloistered man of books. The mass of the people think in the same sort of strong, large, elemental terms as did Sunday. The niceties of language do not bother them; they are the makers and users of that fluid speech called slang.

Wlliam A. Sunday was elemental. Sophistication would have spoiled him. He was dead sure of a few truths of first magnitude. He believed without reservation or qualification in the Christ who saved him and reversed his life's direction. Upon this theme he preached to millions. Also he was sure that there is a devil, and he rather delighted in telling old Satan out loud what he thought of him. Meanness, in Satan, sinner or saint, he hated and said so in the language of the street, which the common people understood. He usually perturbed some fastidious folk who thought that literary culture and religion are essentially interwoven.

Excoriation of the devil was not Sunday's masterpiece. He reached his height in exaltation of Jesus Christ. He was surer of his Lord than he was of the devil. It was his bed-rock belief that Jesus can save anybody, from the gutter habitué to the soul-calloused, wealthy man of the world, and make them both new creatures. With heart tenderness and really yearning love he held aloft the Crucified Christ as the world's only hope. That is why his gospel broke hearts of stone and made Bible-studying, praying church workers out of strange assortments of humanity.

The following passages will show how familiarly and frequently Sunday spoke of the devil:

The devil isn't anybody's fool. You can bank on that. Plenty of folks will tell you there isn't any devil—that he is just a figure of speech; a poetic personification of the sin in our natures. People who say that—and especially all the time-serving, hypocritical ministers who say it—are liars. They are calling the Holy Bible a lie. I'll believe the Bible before I'll believe a lot of time-serving, society-fied, tea-drinking, smirking preachers. No, sir! You take God's Word for it, there is a devil, and a big one, too.

Oh, but the devil is smooth! He always was, and he is now. He is right on his job all the time, winter and summer. Just as he appeared to Christ in the wilderness, he is right in this tabernacle, trying to make sinners indifferent to Christ's sacrifice for salvation. When the invitation is given, and you start to get up, then settle back into your seat, and say, "I guess I don't want to give way to a temporary impulse," that's the real, genuine, blazing-eyed, cloven-hoofed, forked-tailed old devil, hanging to your coat tail. He knows all your weaknesses, and how to appeal to them.

He knows about you and how you have spent sixty dollars in the last two years for tobacco, to make your home and the streets filthy, and that you have not bought your wife a new dress in two years, because you "can't afford it"; and he knows about you, and the time and money you spend on fool hats and card parties, doing what you call "getting into society," while your husband is being driven away from home by badly cooked meals, your children are running on the streets, learning to be hoodlums.

And he knows about you, too, sir, and what you get when you go back of the drug-store prescription counter to "buy medicine for your sick baby." And he knows about you and the lie you told about the girl across the street, because she is sweeter and truer than you are, and the boys go to see her and keep away from you, you miserable thrower of slime, dug out of your own heart of envy—yes, indeed, the devil knows all about you.

When the revival comes along and the church of God gets busy, you will always find the devil gets busy, too. Whenever you find somebody that doesn't believe in the devil you can bank on it that he has a devil in him bigger than a woodchuck. When the Holy Spirit descended at Pentecost the devil didn't do a thing but go around and say that these fellows were drunk. Peter got up and made him mad by saying that it was too early in the day; it was but the third hour. They had sense in those days; it was unreasonable to find them drunk at the third hour of the day. But now fools sit up all night with booze.

When you rush forward in God's work, the devil begins to rush against you. A rustic farmer walking through Lincoln Park, Chicago, saw the sign, "Beware of pickpockets."

"Why do they want to put up a sign like that? Everybody looks honest to me." He reached for his watch to see what time it was and found it gone. The pickpockets always get in the pockets of those who think there are no pickpockets. Whenever you believe there is a devil around, you can keep him out, but if you say there isn't, he'll get you sure.

The Bible says there is a devil; you say there is no devil. Who knows the most, God or you? Jesus met a real foe, a personal devil. Reject it or deny it as you may. If there is no devil, why do you cuss instead of pray? Why do you lie instead of telling the truth? Why don't you kiss your wife instead of cursing her? You have just got the devil in you, that is all.

The devil is no fool; he is on his job. The devil has been practicing for six thousand years and he has never had appendicitis, rheumatism or tonsilitis. If you get to playing tag with the devil he'll beat you every clip.

If I knew that all the devils in Hell and all the devils in Pittsburgh were sitting out in the pews and sneering and jeering at me I'd shoot God's truth into their carcasses anyway. I propose to keep firing away at the devils until by and by they come crawling out of their holes and swear that they were never in them, but their old hides would assay for lead and tan for chair bottoms.

Men in general think very little of the devil and his devices, yet he is the most formidable enemy the human race has to contend with. There is only one attitude to have toward him, and that is to hit him. Don't pick up a sentence and smooth it and polish it and sugar-coat it, but shy it at him with all the rough corners on it.

The devil has more sense than lots of little preachers.

Jesus said: "It is written." He didn't get up and quote Byron and Shakespeare. You get up and quote them and the devil will give you the ha! ha! until you're gray-haired. Give him the Word of God, and he will take the count mighty quick. "It is written, thou shall not tempt the Lord thy God."

Don't you ever think for a minute that the devil isn't on the job all the time. He has been rehearsing for thousands of years. When you fool around in his back yard he will pat you on the back and tell you that you are "IT."

I'll fight the devil in my own way and I don't want people to growl that I am not doing it right.

The devil comes to me sometimes. Don't think that because I am a preacher the devil doesn't bother me. The devil comes around regularly, and I put on the gloves and get busy right away.

I owe God everything; I owe the devil nothing except the best fight I can put up.

I assault the devil's stronghold and I expect no quarter and I give him none.

I am in favor of everything the devil is against, and I am against everything the devil is in favor of—the dance, the booze, the brewery, my friends who have cards in their homes. I am against everything that the devil is in favor of, and I favor everything the devil is against, no matter what it is. If you know which side the devil is on, put me down on the other side any time.

Hell is the highest reward that the devil can offer you for being a servant of his.

The devil has a lot more sense than some of you preachers, and a lot of you old skeptics, who quote Shakespeare and Carlyle and Emerson and everybody and everything rather than the Bible.

When you hear a preacher say that he doesn't believe there is a devil, you can just bet your hat that he never preaches repentance. The men who do any preaching on repentance know there is a devil, for they hear him roar.

I drive the same kind of nails all orthodox preachers do. The only difference is that they use a tack hammer and I use a sledge.

The preacher of today who is a humanitarian question point is preaching to empty benches.

I do not want to believe and preach a lie. I would rather believe and preach a truth, no matter how unpleasant it is. I believe there is a Hell. If I didn't I wouldn't have the audacity to stand up here and preach to you. If there ever comes a time when I don't believe in Hell I will leave the platform before I will ever preach a sermon with that unbelief in my heart. I would rather believe and preach a truth, no matter how unpleasant, than to believe and preach a lie simply for the friendship and favor of some people.

The man who preaches the truth is your friend. I have no desire to be any more broad or liberal than Jesus, not a whit, and nobody has any right either, and claim to be a preacher. Is a man cruel that tells you the truth? The man that tells you there is no Hell is the cruel man, and the man that tells you there is a Hell is your friend. So it's a kindness to point out danger. God's ministers have no business to hold back the truth.

I don't believe you can remember when you heard a sermon on Hell. Well, you'll hear about Hell while I am here. God Almighty put Hell in the Bible and any preacher that sidesteps it because there are people sitting in the pews who don't like it, ought to get out of the pulpit. He is simply trimming his sails to catch a passing breeze of popularity.

CHAPTER 16

CRITICS AND CRITICISM

Some preachers need the cushions of their chairs upholstered oftener than they need their shoes half-soled—"BILLY" SUNDAY.

IT IS ONLY when the bull's-eye is hit that the bell rings. The preacher who never gets a roar out of the forces of unrighteousness may well question whether he is shooting straight. One of the most significant tributes to the Evangelist Sunday was the storm of criticism which raged about his head. It is clear that at least he and his message were not a negligible quantity.

This book holds no brief for the impeccability and invulnerability of "Billy" Sunday. We cannot be blind to the fact he created more commotion in the camp of evil than any other preacher of his generation. Christians were bound to say, "We love him for the enemies he made. He did hit harder at all the forces that hurt humanity and hinder godliness than any other then living warrior of God.

The forces of evil paid "Billy" Sunday the compliment of an elaborately organized and abundantly financed assault. He was usually preceded and followed in his campaigns by systematic attacks which aimed to undermine and discredit him. A weekly paper, issued in Chicago, appeared to be devoted wholly to the disparaging of Mr. Sunday.

In rather startling juxtaposition to that statement is the other that many ministers publicly attacked Sunday. This was clearly within their right. He was a public issue and fairly in controversy. As he claimed the right of free speech for himself he could not deny it to others. Some of his critics among the clergy objected to evangelism in general, some to his particular methods, some to his forms of speech, some to his theology; but no one apparently objected to his results.

Whatever "Billy" Sunday's shortcomings, he was unquestionably an ally of the kingdom of Heaven and an enemy of sin. His motives and his achievements were both aligned on the side of Christ and His Church. A host of ministers of fine judgment who were grieved by some of the evangelist's forms of speech and some of his methods, withheld their voices from criticism because they did not want to fire upon the kingdom's warriors from the rear. Sunday got results for God; therefore, reasoned they, why should they attack him?

There was no religious leader who had such a host of ardent defenders and supporters as "Billy" Sunday. The enthusiasm of myriads for this man was second only to their devotion to Christ. Wherever he went he left behind him a militant body of protagonists. He was championed valiantly and fearlessly.

So vigorous was this spirit which followed in the wake of a Sunday campaign that in a certain large city where the ministers of one denomination had publicly issued a statement disapproving of Mr.

Sunday, their denomination later suffered seriously in public estimation.

Some anonymous supporter of "Billy" Sunday issued a pamphlet made up exclusively of quotations from Scripture justifying Sunday and his message. He quoted such pertinent words as these:

> And I, brethren, when I came to you, came not with excellency of speech or of wisdom, declaring unto you the testimony of God.
>
> For I determined not to know any thing among you, save Jesus Christ, and him crucified.
>
> And I was with you in weakness, and in fear, and in much trembling.
>
> And my speech and my preaching was not with enticing words of man's wisdom, but in demonstration of the Spirit and of power:

A great marvel was that this unconventional preacher enlisted among his supporters a host of intellectual and spiritual leaders. The churches of the country, broadly speaking, were for him, and so were their pastors. This might be attributed to partisanship, for certainly Sunday was promoting the work of the church; but what was to be said when Provost Edgar F. Smith of the University of Pennsylvania came out in an unqualified endorsement of the man and his work; or such an acute lawyer and distinguished churchman as George Wharton Pepper of Philadelphia, well known in the councils of the Protestant Episcopal Church, gave his hearty approval to Sunday?

Consider the letter which Secretary of State Bryan wrote to Sunday after hearing him at Pittsburgh:

THE SECRETARY OF STATE

Washington, January 12, 1914.

MY DEAR SUNDAY: Having about four hours in Pittsburgh last night, my wife and I attended your meeting and so we heard and felt the powerful sermon which you delivered. We noted the attention of that vast audience and watched the people, men and women, old and young, who thronged about you in response to your appeal. Mrs. Bryan had never heard you, and I had heard only a short afternoon address. Last night you were at your best. I cannot conceive of your surpassing that effort in effectiveness.

Do not allow yourself to be disturbed by criticism. God is giving you souls for your hire and that is a sufficient answer. Christ called attention to the fact that both he and John the Baptist had to meet criticism because they were so much unlike in manner. No man can do good without making enemies, but yours as a rule will be among those who do not hear you. Go on, and may the heavenly Father use you for many years to come, as He has for many years past, and bring multitudes to know Christ as He presented Himself when He said, "I am the way, the truth and the life."

Am sorry we could not see you personally, but we left because we found that we were discovered. Some insisted upon shaking hands and I was afraid I might become a cause of disturbance. Mrs. Bryan joins me in regards to Mrs. Sunday and yourself.

Yours truly,

W. J. BRYAN

One need be surprised at nothing in connection with such a personality as "Billy" Sunday, yet surely there was no precedent for this resolution, adopted by the Pittsburgh City Council, while he was in that city:

WHEREAS, The Rev. William A. Sunday and his party have been in the city of Pittsburgh for the past eight weeks, conducting evangelistic services, and the Council of the city being convinced of the immense good which has been accomplished through his work for morality, good citizenship and religion, therefore be it

Resolved, That the Council of the city of Pittsburgh express its utmost confidence in Mr. Sunday and all of the members of his party; and be it further

Resolved, That it does hereby express to them its appreciation of all the work that has been done, and extends to Mr. Sunday its most cordial wishes for his future success.

While the adverse critics did all in their power to discredit him as he went from place to place, Sunday's friends also were not idle. In Scranton, for instance, before the campaign opened, men in nearly all walks of life received letters from men in corresponding callings in Pittsburgh bearing tribute to "Billy" Sunday. Bankers would enclose in their correspondence from Pittsburgh an earnest recommendation of Sunday and a suggestion that the bankers of Scranton stand squarely to his support. The local Scranton plumber heard from a plumbers' supply house; labor union men heard from their fellows in Pittsburgh; lawyers and doctors, and a host of businessmen, had letters from personal friends in Pittsburgh, telling what Sunday had done for that community, and in many cases bearing personal testimony to what his message had meant to the writers.

This is nearer to effective organization than the Christian forces of the country commonly get. This form of propaganda did not bulk large in the public eye, but it created a splendid undercurrent of sentiment; for banker Jones could say: "I have it straight from banker Smith of Pittsburgh, whom I know to be a level-headed man, that Sunday is all right, and that he does nothing but good for the city."

Still more novel than this was the expedition sent by a great daily newspaper to hear the evangelist in Scranton. There was no parallel in the history of Christian work for the deputation of more than two hundred pastors who went to Scranton from Philadelphia. These went entirely at the charges of the Philadelphia *North American,* being carried in special trains. The railroad company recognized the significance of this unusual occasion, and both ways the train broke records for speed.

While in the city of Scranton the ministers were the guests of the Scranton churches. They had special space reserved for them in the tabernacle and their presence drew the greatest crowds that were experienced during the Scranton campaign. Of course thousands were turned away. Nobody who saw and heard it will forget the way that solid block of Philadelphia pastors stood up and sang "I Love to Tell the Story."

Between sessions these Philadelphia ministers were visiting their brethren in Scranton, learning in most detailed fashion what the effects of the Sunday campaign had been. Whenever they gathered in public assemblies they sounded the refrain, which grew in significance from day to day: "I Love to Tell the Story." Sunday fired the evangelistic purpose of these pastors.

When this unique excursion was ended, and the company had detrained at the Reading Terminal, the ministers, without prearrangement, gathered in a body in the train shed and lifted their voices in the refrain "I Love to Tell the Story," while hundreds and thousands of hurrying city folk, attracted by the music, gathered to learn what this could possibly mean.

A new militancy was put into the preaching of these clergymen by their Scranton visit; and many of them later reported that the largest congregations of all their ministerial experience were those which gathered to hear them report on the Sunday evangelistic campaign. Not a few of the preachers had to repeat "Billy" Sunday sermons. Needless to say, an enthusiastic and urgent invitation to Sunday to go to Philadelphia to conduct a campaign followed this demonstration on the part of the daily newspaper.

That there is a strategic value in rallying all the churches about one man was demonstrated by the Methodists of Philadelphia. Bishop Joseph F. Berry had heartily indorsed the project, and had urged all of the Methodist pastors who could possibly do so to accept the *North American's* invitation. The Methodist delegation was an enthusiastic unit. When they returned to Philadelphia a special issue of the local Methodist paper was issued. Thirty-two articles appeared, each written by an aroused pastor who had been a member of the delegation. Incidentally, all of the city papers, as well as the religious press of a very wide region, reported this extraordinary pilgrimage of more than two hundred pastors to a distant city to hear an evangelist preach. A reflex of this was the return visit, some months later, of a thousand "trail-hitters" to speak in Philadelphia pulpits.

Before leaving the subject of the criticism of Sunday, pro and con, it should be insisted that no public man or institution should be free from the corrective power of public opinion, openly expressed. This is one of the wholesome agencies of democracy. Mr. Sunday himself was not slow to express his candid opinion of the church, the ministry, and of society at large. It would have been a sad day for him if all critical judgment upon his work had given way to unreasoning adulation.

The best rule to follow is, "Never judge unfinished work." Only a completed campaign should pass in review before the critics; only the whole substance of the man's message; only the entire effect of his work upon the public. Partial judgments are sure to be incorrect.

"Billy" Sunday succeeded in making clear to all his hearers—indeed he impressed them so deeply that the whole city talked of little else for weeks—that God has dealings with every man; and that God cares enough about man to provide for him a way of escape from the terrible reality of sin, that Way being Jesus Christ.

When a preacher succeeds in lodging that conviction in the minds of the multitude, he is Heaven's messenger. Whether he speaks in Choctaw, Yiddish, Bostonese or in slang, is too trivial a matter to discuss. We do not inspect the wardrobe or the vocabulary of the hero who rides before the flood, urging the people to safety in the hills.

CHAPTER 17

MAKING A JOYFUL NOISE

Don't look as if your religion hurt you—"BILLY" SUNDAY.

H E HATH PUT A NEW SONG in my mouth." That is real religion which sets the saints to singing. Gloomy Christians are a poor advertisement of the Gospel. There was nothing of gloom about a Sunday revival.

Shrewd students of the campaigns often remarked that there were a few tears and much laughter at the evangelist's services. There was scarcely one of Sunday's sermons in which he did not make the congregation laugh. All of his work was attuned to the note of vitality, robustness and happiness. Concerning the long-faced Christian, Sunday said:

"Some people couldn't have faces any longer if they thought God was dead. They ought to pray to stop looking so sour. If they smile it looks like it hurts them, and you're always glad when they stop smiling. If Paul and Silas had had such long faces, as some church members have on them, when they went into the Philippian jail, the jailer would never have been saved. There never was a greater mistake than to suppose that God wants you to be long-faced when you put on your good clothes. You'd better not fast at all if you give the devil all the benefit. God wants people to be happy.

"The matter with a lot of you people is that your religion is not complete. You have not yielded yourself to God and gone out for God and God's truth. Why, I am almost afraid to make some folks laugh for fear that I will be arrested for breaking a costly piece of antique bric-a-brac. You would think that if some people laughed it would break their faces. I want to tell you that the happy, smiling, sunny-faced religion will win more people to Jesus Christ than the miserable old grimfaced kind will in ten years. I pity any one who can't laugh. There must be something wrong with their religion or their liver. The devil can't laugh.

"Don't look as if religion hurt. Don't look as if you had on a number two shoe when you ought to be wearing a number five. I see some women who look as if they had the toothache. That won't win anyone for Christ. Look pleasant. Look as if religion made you happy.

"Then there is music. When you get to Heaven you'll find that not all have been preached there. They have been sung there. God pity us when music is not for the glory of God. Some of you will sing for money and for honor, but you won't sing in the church. Some of these high-priced sopranos get up in church and do a little diaphragm wiggle and make a noise like a horse neighing. I don't wonder the people in the congregation have a hard time of it."

Mr. Sunday set the city to singing. His sermons were framed in music—and not music that was a performance by some soloist, but music that ministered to his message. His gospel was sung as well as preached. The singing was as essential a part of the service as the sermon. Everybody likes good music, especially of a popular sort. Sunday saw that this taste was gratified.

The tabernacle music in itself was enough to draw the great throngs which nightly crowded the building. The choir furnished not only the melodies but also a rare spectacle. This splendid regiment of helpers seated back of the speaker affected both the eyes and the ears of the audiences. Without his choirs Sunday could scarcely conduct his great campaigns. These helpers were all volunteers. Their steadfast loyalty throughout weeks of strenuous meetings in all kinds of weather was a Christian service of the first order.

True, membership in a Sunday choir was in itself an avocation, a social and religious interest that enriched the lives of the choir members. They "belonged" to something big and popular. They had new themes for conversation. New acquaintances were made. The associations first formed in the Sunday choir have in many cases continued as the most sacred relations of life. The brightest spot in the monotony of many a young person's life was his or her membership in the "Billy" Sunday choir.

The choir also had the advantage of a musical drill and experience which could be secured in no other way. All the advantages of trained leadership were given in return for the volunteer service. Incidentally, the choir members knew that they were serving their churches and their communities in a deep and far-reaching fashion.

Many visitors to the Sunday tabernacle were surprised to find that the music was of fine quality. There was less "religious rag-time" than was commonly associated with the idea of revival meetings.

More than a fair half of the music sung was that
which holds an established place in the hymnody
of all churches.

There was more to the music of a campaign than
the volume of singing by the choir, with an occasional solo by the chorister or some chosen person.
A variety of ingenious devices were employed to
heighten the impression of the music. Thus a common antiphonal effect was obtained by having the
choir sing one line of a hymn and the last ten rows
of persons in the rear of the tabernacle sing the
answering line. The old hymn "For You I Am Praying" was used with electrical effect in this. Part
singing was employed in ways possible only to
such a large chorus as the musical director of the
Sunday campaigns had at his command.

A genius for mutuality characterized the Sunday
song services. The audience was given a share in the
music. Not only were they requested to join in the
singing, but they were permitted to choose their
favorite hymns, and frequently the choir was called
upon to listen while the audience sang.

Various delegations were permitted to sing hymns
of their own choice. Diversity, and variety and vim
seem to be the objective of the musical part of the
program. From half an hour to an hour of this
varied music introduced each service. When the
evangelist himself was ready to preach, the crowd
had been worked up into a glow and fervor that
made it receptive to his message.

If some stickler for ritual and stateliness objects
that these services were entirely too informal, and
too much like a political campaign, the partisan of
Mr. Sunday will heartily assent. These were great
American crowds in their everyday humor. These
evangelistic meetings were not regular church services. It has already been made plain that there was

no "dim religious light" about the Sunday tabernacle meetings.

It was a tribute to the comprehensiveness of the Sunday method that they brought together the most representative gatherings imaginable every day under the unadorned rafters of the big wooden shell called the tabernacle. Shrewdly, the evangelist made sure of the democratic quality of his congregation. He had succeeded in having the gospel sing its way into the affection and interest of everyday folk.

It was no valid objection to the Sunday music that it was so thoroughly entertaining. The tabernacle crowds sang, not as a religious duty, but for the sheer joy of singing. One of the commonest remarks heard was "I never expect to hear such singing again till I get to Heaven." It is real Christian ministry to put the melodies of the gospel into the memories of multitudes, and to brighten with the songs of salvation the gray days of the burdenbearers of the world. Boys and men on the street whistled gospel songs. The echoes of tabernacle music could be heard long after Mr. Sunday had gone from a community. This is the strategy of "the expulsive power of a new affection." These meetings gave to Christians a new and jubilant affirmation, instead of a mere defense for their faith. The campaign music carried the campaign message farther than the voice of any man could ever penetrate.

CHAPTER 18

THE PROPHET AND HIS OWN TIME

There wouldn't be so many non-church goers if there were not so many non-going churches— "BILLY" SUNDAY.

A PROPHET to his own generation was Mr. Sunday. In the speech of the day he arraigned the sins of the day and sought to satisfy the needs of the day. A man singularly free and fearless, he applied the Gospel to the conditions of the moment. Knowing life on various levels, he preached with a definiteness and an appropriateness that echoed the prophet Nathan's "Thou art the man." By the very structure of "Billy" Sunday's mentality it was made difficult for him to be abstract. He had to deal definitely with concrete sins.

Now a pastor would find it difficult to approach, in the ruthless and reckless fashion of "Billy" Sunday, the shortcomings of his members and neighbors. He has to live with his congregation, year in and year out; but the evangelist is as irresponsible as John the Baptist on the banks of the Jordan. He has no affiliations to consider and no consequences to fear, except the kingdom's welfare. His only concern is for the truth and applicability of his message. He is perfectly heedless about offending hearers. Well-meaning persons who compare "Billy" Sunday with the average pastor should bear this in mind.

A rare gift of satire and scorn and invective and ridicule had been given to Sunday. He had been equipped with powerful weapons which are too often missing from the armory of the average gospel soldier. His aptitude for puncturing sham was almost unique in contemporary life. Few orators in any field had his art of heaping up adjectives to a towering height that overwhelmed their objective.

Nor did the church escape Sunday's plain dealing. He treated vigorously her shortcomings and her imperfections. Usually, the persons who heard the first half dozen or dozen sermons in one of his campaigns were shocked by the reckless way in which the evangelist handled the church and church members.

Others, forewarned, perceived the psychology of it. It was clear that in Sunday's thinking the purity of the church was all-important. Complacency with any degree of corruption or inefficiency on her part he regarded as sin. So he unsparingly belabored the church and her ministry for all the good that they left undone and all amiss that they had done.

The net result of this was that the evangelist left on the minds of the multitudes, to whom the church has been a negligible quantity, a tremendous impression of her pre-eminent importance. It was true that sometimes, after a Sunday campaign, a few ministers had to leave their churches, because of the new spirit of efficiency and spirituality which he imparted. They were simply unable to measure up to the new opportunity. On the whole, however, it was clear that he imparted a new sense of dignity and a new field of leadership to the ministers of the gospel in the communities he served.

*   *   *

Concerning the prayers of Sunday there is little to be said except to let the reader judge for himself.

That they were unconventional no one will deny; many have gone farther and have said that they were almost sacrilegious. The charge was often made that the evangelist addressed his prayers to the crowd instead of to God. No one criticism was oftener made of Mr. Sunday by sensitive and thoughtful ministers of the Gospel, than that his public prayers seemed to be lacking in fundamental reverence.

The defender of Sunday rejoined, "He talks to Jesus as familiarly as he talks to one of his associates." Really, though, there is deep difference. His fellow workers are only fellow workers, but of the Lord, "Holy and reverend is His name." Many of the warmest admirers of the evangelist did not attempt to defend all of his prayers.

Probably Sunday did not know that in all the Oriental, and some European, languages there is a special form of speech reserved for royalty; that it would be an affront to address a king by the same term as the commoner. The outward signs of this mental attitude of reverence in prayer were unquestionably lacking in Sunday.

His usual procedure was to begin to pray at the end of a sermon, without any interval or any prefatory remarks, such as "Let us pray." For an instant, the crowd did not realize that he was praying. He closed his eyes and said, "Now Jesus, you know," and so forth, just as he would say to his chorister, "Rody, what is the name of that delegation?" He interjected just this inquiry into a prayer. Or he mentioned "that Bible class over to my right, near the platform." He used the same colloquial figures of speech in a prayer—baseball phrases, for instance —that he did in his sermons. Sometimes it was really difficult to tell whether he was addressing the Lord or the audience.

More direct familiar, childish petitions were never addressed to the Deity than were heard at the Sunday meetings. They ran so counter to all religious conceptions of a reverential approach to the throne of grace that one marveled at the charity of the ministers in letting him go unrebuked. But they said "It's 'Billy,'" and so it was. That is the way the man prayed in private, in his own room, before starting out to preach; and in entirely the same intimate, unconventional fashion he asked the help of Jesus in his preaching and in the meetings. But to the prayers themselves:

"O God, help this old world. May the men who have been drunkards be made better; may the men who beat their wives and curse their children come to Jesus; may the children who have feared to hear the footsteps of their father rejoice again when they see the parent coming up the steps of the home. Bring the church up to help the work. Bless them, Lord. Bless the preachers: bless the officials of the church and bless everyone in them. Save the men in the mines. Save the poor breaker boys as they toil day by day in dangers; save them for their mothers and fathers and bring them to Jesus. Bless the policemen, the newspapermen and the men, women and children; the men and girls from the plants, factories, stores and streets. Go into the stores every morning and have prayer meetings so that the clerks may hear the Word of God before they get behind the counters and sell goods to the trade.

"Visit this city, O Lord, its schools and scholars, and bless the school board. Bless the city officials. Go down into the city hall and bless the mayor, directors and all the rest. We thank Thee that the storm has passed. We believe that we will learn a lesson of how helpless we are before Thee. How chesty we are when the sun shines and the day is clear, but, oh! how helpless when the breath of God comes and the snowflakes start to fall; when the floods come we get on our knees and wring our hands and ask mercy from Thee. Oh, help us, O Lord.

"When the people get to Hell—I hope that nobody will ever go there and I am trying my best to save them—they will know that they are there because they lived against God. I am not here to injure them; I am not here to wreck homes; I am here to tell them of the blessing You send down when they are with You. We pray for the thousands and thousands that will be saved."

*   *   *

"O Lord, there are a lot of people who step up to the collection plate at church and fan. And Lord, there are always people sitting in the grandstand and calling the batter a mutt. He can't hit a thing or he can't get it over the base, or he's an ice wagon on the bases, they say. O Lord, give us some coachers out at this tabernacle so that people can be brought Home to you. Some of them are dying on second and third base, Lord, and we don't want that. Lord, have the people play the game of life right up to the limit so that home runs may be scored. There are some people, Lord, who say, 'Yes, I have heard Billy at the tabernacle and oh, it is so disgusting: really it's awful the way he talks.' Lord, if there weren't some grouches and the like in the city I'd be lost. We had a grand meeting last night,

Lord, when the crowd came down from Dickson-ville (or what was that place, Rody?), Dickson City, Lord, that's right. It was a great crowd. There's an undercurrent of religion sweeping through here, Lord, and we are getting along fine.

"There are some dandy folks in Scranton, lots of good men and women that are with us in this campaign, and Lord, we want You to help make this a wonderful campaign. It has been wonderful so far. Lord, it's great to see them pouring in here night after night. God, you have the people of the homes tell their maids to go to the meeting at the Y. W. C. A. Thursday afternoon, and God, let us have a crowd of the children here Saturday. Rody is going to talk to them, Lord. He can't preach and I can't sing, but the children will have a big time with him, Lord. Lord, I won't try to stop people from roasting and scoring me. I would not know what to do if I didn't get some cracks from people now and then."

*　　*　　*

"Well, Jesus, I don't know how to talk as I would like to talk. I am at a loss as to just what to say tonight. Father, if you hadn't provided salvation, we'd all be pretty badly off. Knowing the kind of life I live and the kind of lives other people live, I know you are very patient and kind, but if you can do for men and women what you did for me, I wish it would happen. I wouldn't dare stand up and say that I didn't believe in You. I'd be afraid You would paralyze me or take away my mind. I'm afraid you would do that. There are hundreds here tonight who don't know You as their Saviour. The Bible class believes You are Jesus of Nazareth, but they don't know You as a personal Saviour. And these other delegations, Lord, help them all to come down. Well, well, well, it's wonderful—'I find no fault in Him.' Amen."

CHAPTER 19

THE REVIVAL ON TRIAL

One spark of fire can do more to prove the power of powder than a whole library written on the subject—"BILLY" SUNDAY.

IT IS COMMON TO OBJECT to revivals and to revivalists. Sunday's reply to this was simply unanswerable: he appealed to the people themselves for evidence. By a show of hands—and he conducted this experiment in practically every community he visited—he gave a convincing demonstration that it is by special evangelistic efforts that most Christians have entered the church of Christ. By the same method, he showed that youth is the time to make the great decision.

When this question was put to a test a dramatic moment, the significance of which the multitude quickly grasps, ensued. On occasion there were more than twenty thousand persons within the tabernacle. First the evangelist asked the confessed Christians to rise. The great bulk of the congregation stood on its feet. Then he asked for those who were converted in special meetings, revivals of some sort or other, to raise their hands. From three-fourths to four-fifths of the persons standing lifted their hands in token that they were converted during revivals.

Then—each time elaborating his question so that there would be no misunderstanding—Sunday asked those who were converted before they were twenty to indicate it by sitting down. Here again the majority was so large as to be simply overwhelming. It almost seemed that the whole body of Christians had become such before they attained their legal majority.

Of the few hundreds that were left standing, Sunday asked in turn for those who were converted after they were thirty, those who were converted after they were forty, before they were fifty, after they were sixty. When it came to this point of age the scene was thrilling in its significance. Usually there were only one or two persons standing who entered the Christian life after reaching fifty years of age.

The conclusion is irresistible. (Unless a person accepts Christ in youth the chances are enormously against his ever accepting Him.) The demonstration was argument of the importance of an early decision for Christ.

After such a showing, everybody was willing to listen to a sermon on revivals and their place in the economy of the kingdom of Heaven.

* * *

The oldest problem of the Christian church, and the latest problem of democracy, is how to reach the great masses of people. Frequently the charge is made that the church merely skims the surface of society, and that the great uncaring masses of the people lie untouched beneath it. Commonly, a revival reaches only a short distance outside the cir-

cumference of church circles. The wonder and
greatness of the "Billy" Sunday campaigns consisted
in the fact that they reached to the uttermost rim
of a community, to its greatest height and its lowest
depth. There can be no question that he stirred a
city as not even the fiercest political campaign did.
Sunday touched life on all levels, bringing his message to bear upon the society woman in her parlor
and the humblest day laborer in a trench.

This did not come to pass by any mere chance.
Organized activity achieved it. The method which
produced the greatest results is what is called the
delegation idea, whereby detachments of persons
from various trades, callings and organizations and
communities attended in a body upon the services
of the Sunday tabernacle.

By prearrangement, seats were reserved every
night for visiting delegations. Sometimes there were
as many as a dozen delegations present in one evening. As the campaign progressed toward its conclusion real difficulty was experienced in finding
open dates for all the delegations that applied. At
the outset, Mr. Sunday's assistants had to "work up"
these delegations. Later, the delegations themselves
sought the workers.

In variety the delegations ranged from a regiment
of Boy Scouts to a post of old soldiers; from the
miners of a specified colliery to the bankers of the
city; from the telephone girls to the members of a
woman's club; from an athletic club to a Bible class.

Not only the community in which the meetings
were being held furnished these delegations, but the
surrounding territory was drawn upon. It was by
no means an unknown thing for a single delegation,
numbering a thousand or fifteen hundred men, to
come a distance of fifteen or twenty-five miles to attend a service. Almost every evening there were

lines of special cars waiting for these deputations who came from afar, with banners and badges and bands, all bent upon hearing and being heard at the tabernacle.

The crowd-spirit was appealed to by this method. The everyday instinct of loyalty to one's craft or crowd was aroused. Each delegation felt its own identity and solidarity, and wanted to make as good a showing as possible. There was considerable wholesome emulation among the delegations representing the same craft or community. Of course, the work of making ready the delegation furnished a topic for what is literally "shop talk" among working men. Naturally each group zealously watched the effect of its appearance upon the great congregation. Delegations get a very good idea of what their neighbors think of them by the amount of applause with which they are greeted. Thus when the whole force of a daily newspaper appeared in the tabernacle its readers cheered vociferously. Every delegation went equipped with its own battle cry, and prepared to make as favorable a showing as possible.

All this is wholesome for community life. It fosters loyalty in the varied groups that go to make up society. Any shop is the better for its workers, led by their heads of departments and by their employers, having gone in a solid phalanx to a tabernacle meeting. Every incident of that experience becomes an unfailing source of conversation for long days and weeks to follow.

Naturally, too, each delegation, delighted with the showing it had made at the tabernacle, and with the part it had borne in the meeting, became one more group of partisans for the Sunday campaign. Men who would not go alone to the tabernacle, could not in loyalty well refuse to stand by their own crowd. So it came to pass that the delegation idea penetrated every level and every section of the community. A shrewder scheme for reaching the last man could scarcely have been devised. Thousands impervious to religious appeals quickly responded to the request that they stand by their shopmates and associates.

Participation in the meetings made the people themselves feel the importance of their part. They were not merely a crowd coming to be talked at; they shared in the meetings. The newspapers commented upon them even as upon the sermon. All were uplifted by the glow of geniality and camaraderie which pervaded the tabernacle. For the songs and slogans and banners of the delegations greatly helped to swell the interest.

All this was wholesome, democratic and typically American. This good-natured crowd did not become unreal or artificial simply because it was facing the fundamental verities of the human soul.

Outspoken loyalty, a characteristic of Sunday converts, expressed itself through many channels. Taught by the delegation idea, as well as by the sermon, the importance of standing up to be counted, the friends and converts of the evangelist were always ready for the great parade which usually was held toward the close of the campaign. The simple basis for this street demonstration was found in the old Scripture, "Let the redeemed of the Lord say so." The idea of the Roman imperial triumph survived in the "Billy" Sunday parade. It was a testimony to the multitudes of the loyalty of Christians to the gospel.

Beyond all question, a tremendous impression was made upon a city by the thousands of marching men whom the evangelist first led and then reviewed. A street parade is a visualization of the forces of the church in a community. Many a man of the street, who might be unmoved by many arguments, however powerful, cannot escape the impression of the might of the massed multitudes of men who march through the streets, thousands strong. Some twenty thousand men were in the Sunday parade at Scranton. Nobody who witnessed them, be he a heedless scoffer, could again speak slightingly of the church. Religion lost whatever traits of femininity it may have possessed, before the Sunday campaign was over.

Those most practical of men, the politicians, were quick to take cognizance of the new power that had arisen in the community's life. They knew that every one of the men not only had a vote, but was a center of influence for the things in which he believed.

The heartening effect of such a great demonstration upon the obscure, lonely and discouraged saints was beyond calculation.

The great hosts of the "Billy" Sunday campaign were returning to first principles by taking religion out into the highways and making it talked about, even as the Founder of the Church created a commotion in the highways of Capernaum and Jerusalem. These marching men were a sermon one or two miles long. The impression made upon youth was not to be registered by any means in the possession of men. Every Christian the world around must have been grateful to Mr. Sunday and his associates for giving the sort of demonstration, which could be misunderstood by the world at large, of the virility and the immensity of the hosts of Heaven on earth.

Many of the utterances of "Billy" Sunday were attuned to this note of valiant witness-bearing for Christ.

CHAPTER 20

A LIFE ENLISTMENT

When a man, after starting to be a Christian, looks back, it is only a question of time until he goes back—"BILLY" SUNDAY.

PROFESSOR WILLIAM JAMES, the philosopher, contended that there was a scientific value to the stories of Christian conversions; that these properly belonged among the data of religion, to be weighed by the man of science.

This point is one of the most critical in the whole realm of the discussion of revivals. Times without number it has been charged that the converts of evangelists lose their religion as quickly as they got it. A perfectly fair question to ask concerning "Billy" Sunday campaigns was, "Were they temporary attacks of religious hysteria, mere effervescent moods of spiritual exaltation, which were dissipated by the first contact with life's realities?"

Here was opportunity for the acid test. "Billy" Sunday conducted revival meetings long enough to enable an investigator to go back over his trail and trace results. After years passed, were there still evidences of the presence and work of the evangelist? The most skeptical and antagonistic person could not fail to find hundreds and thousands of "Billy" Sunday converts in the churches of the towns where the evangelist conducted meetings.

Not all of the converts held fast; we cannot forget that one of the twelve was a complete renegade, and that the others were for a time weak in the faith. Alas, this condition is true of Christian converts. The terrible record revealed in each year's church statistics of members who are missing—entirely lost to the knowledge of the church—is enough to restrain every pastor from making uncharitable remarks about the recruits won by an evangelist. The fact to be stressed was and is that "Billy" Sunday converts were found in all departments of church work, in the ministry itself, and on the foreign field.

One reason for the conservation of the results of the Sunday campaigns was that all the powers of the evangelist and his organization were exerted to lead those who confessed Christ in the tabernacles to become members of the church of their choice, at the earliest possible date. Sunday said candidly that converts cannot expect to grow in grace and usefulness outside the organized church of Christ. Thus it came about that before a Sunday campaign closed, and for months afterward, the church papers reported wholesale accessions to the local congregations of all denominations. Three thousand new church members were added in a single Sunday in the city of Scranton.

What these campaigns meant in the way of rehabilitating individual churches was illustrated by what a Scranton pastor said toward the close of the Sunday campaign: "You know my church burned down a short time ago. We have been planning to rebuild. Now, however, we shall have to rebuild to twice the size of our old church, and we have enough new members already to make sure that our financial problem will be a simple one." The coming of the evangelist had turned into a triumph and a new starting point for this congregation what might otherwise have been a time of discouragement and temporary defeat.

For a moment the reader should take the viewpoint of the pastors who had been struggling along faithfully, year after year, at best getting but a few score of new members each year. Then Sunday appeared. The entire atmosphere and outlook of the church was transformed within a few days. Optimism reigned. Lax church members became Christian workers, and enthusiasm for the kingdom pervaded the entire membership. The churches of the community found themselves bound together in a new solidarity of fellowship and service.

To crown all, into the church membership came literally hundreds of men and women, mostly young, and all burning with the convert's ardent zeal to do service for the Master. Can anybody but a pastor conceive the thrill that must have come to the minister of a Wilkes-Barre church which added one thousand new members to its existing roll, as a result of the "Billy" Sunday campaign?

There were four Protestant churches in Carbondale, a small town sixteen miles from Scranton, which received a thousand new members within five months. All these converts were either the direct result of Sunday's preaching, or else the converts of converts. Out of a Protestant population of nine thousand persons, the Carbondale churches received one-ninth into their membership within six months. These bare figures did not express the greater total of Christian service and enthusiasm which permeated the community as an abiding legacy of the "Billy" Sunday campaign. These converts considered that they had been saved to serve.

Asked to fix a period after which he would expect a reaction from the Sunday meetings, a critic would probably have said about one year. We learn that when the evangelist visited the city of Scranton which is within an hour's ride of Wilkes-Barre, he found that the influence of the meetings which he had held a year previously in Wilkes-Barre were perhaps the most potent single factor in preparing the people of Scranton for his coming. Night after night Wilkes-Barre sent delegations of scores and hundreds over to the Scranton tabernacle. Investigators from afar who went to look into the Scranton meetings were advised to go to the neighboring city to ascertain what were the effects of the campaign after a year. The result was always convincing.

When the evangelist was in Pittsburgh, McKeesport, where he had been six years before, sent many delegations to hear him. On one occasion fifteen hundred persons made the journey from McKeesport to Pittsburgh to testify to the lasting benefits which their city had received.

Usually some organization of the "trail-hitters" was effected after the evangelist's departure. These were bands for personal Christian work. The most remarkable of them all was reported from Wichita, Kansas, where the aftermath of the Sunday meetings became so formidable as to suggest a new and general method of Christian service by laymen.

The Sunday converts organized themselves into "Gospel Teams," who announced that they were ready to go anywhere and conduct meetings especially for men. They offered to pay their own expenses, although frequently the communities inviting them refused to permit this. Sometimes the gospel teams traveled by automobiles or streetcars and sometimes they made long railway journeys.

There were more than three hundred gospel teams in this work and they formed "The National Federation of Gospel Teams."

Eleven thousand conversions were soon reported by these unsalaried, self-supporting gospel workers, who joyously acclaimed Sunday as their leader. They represented his teachings and his spirit in action.

The most celebrated of these gospel teams was "The Business Men's Team" of Wichita, an interdenominational group. Such men as Henry Allen, the editor of the Wichita *Beacon* and one of the foremost public men of the state; the president of the Interurban Railway; the president of the Kansas Mutual Bank, and other eminent businessmen were in it. This team visited various states in its work, all without a penny of cost to the church, and with results exceeding those achieved by many great and expensive organizations.

The "Billy" Sunday converts not only stayed, but they multiplied and became effective servants of the church and the kingdom.

Nobody was left to conjecture as to the counsel that Mr. Sunday gave converts. Every man, woman and child who "hit the trail" was handed a leaflet, telling him how to make a success of the Christian life.

A trumpet call to Christian service by every confessed disciple of Jesus Christ was sounded by the evangelist. The following is such an appeal:

"SHARP-SHOOTERS"

This century has witnessed two apparently contradictory facts: The decline of the church and the growth of religious hunger in the masses. The world during the nineteenth and early twentieth centuries passed through a period of questionings and doubts, during which everything in Heaven and earth was put into a crucible and melted down into constituent elements. During that period many laymen and preachers lost their moorings.

The definite challenging note was lost out of the life of the ministry. The preacher is often a human interrogation point, preaching to empty pews. The hurrying, busy crowd in the street is saying to the preacher and the church, "When you have something definite to say about the issues of life, Heaven, Hell and salvation, we will listen; till then we have no time for you." The mission of the church is to carry the gospel of Christ to the world.

I believe that lack of efficient personal work is one of the failures of the church today. The people of the church are like squirrels in a cage. Lots of activity, but accomplishing nothing. It doesn't require a Christian life to sell oyster soup or run a bazaar or a rummage sale.

Many churches report no new members on confession of faith. Why these meager results with this tremendous expenditure of energy and money? Why are so few people coming into the kingdom? I will tell you—there is not a definite effort put forth to persuade a definite person to receive a definite Saviour at a definite time, and that definite time is now.

I tell you the church of the future must have personal work and prayer. The trouble with some churches is that they think the preacher is a sort of ecclesiastical locomotive, who will snort and puff and pull the whole bunch through to glory.

A politician will work harder to get a vote than the church of God will work to have men brought to Christ. Watch some of the preachers go down the aisles. They drag along as if they had grindstones tied to their feet.

No political campaign is won solely by a stump speaker or spell-binder on the platform. It is won by a man-to-man canvass.

The Value of Personal Work

The children of this generation are wiser than the

children of light. You can learn something from the world about how to do things. Personal work is the simplest and most effective form of work we can engage in. Andrew wins Peter. Peter wins three thousand at Pentecost. A man went into a boot and shoe store and talked to the clerk about Jesus Christ. He won the clerk to Christ. Do you know who that young man was? It was Dwight L. Moody, and he went out and won multitudes to Christ. The name of the man who won him was Kimball, and Kimball will get as much reward as Moody. Kimball worked to win Moody and Moody worked and won a multitude. Andrew wins Peter and Peter wins three thousand at Pentecost. That is the way God works. Charles G. Finney, after learning the name of any man or woman, would invariably ask: "Are you a Christian?" There is no one here who has not drag enough to win somebody to Christ.

Personal work is a difficult form of work; more difficult than preaching, singing, attending conventions, giving your goods to feed the poor. The devil will let you have an easy time until God asks you to do personal work. It is all right while you sing in the choir, but just as soon as you get out and work for God the devil will be on your back and you will see all the flimsy excuses you can offer for not working for the Lord. If you want to play into the hands of the devil begin to offer your excuses.

There are many people who want to win somebody for Jesus and they are waiting to be told how to do it. I believe there are hundreds and thousands of people who are willing to work and who know something must be done, but they are waiting for help; I mean men and women of ordinary ability. Many people are sick and tired and disgusted with just professing religion; they are tired of trotting to church and trotting home again. They sit in a pew and listen to a sermon; they are tired of that, not speaking to anybody and not engaging in personal work; they are getting tired of it and the church is dying because of it. People should wake up and win souls for Jesus Christ.

I want to say to the deacons, stewards, vestrymen, prudential committees, that they should work, and the place to begin is at your own home. Sit down and write the names of five or ten friends, and many of them members of your own church, and two or three of those not members of any church; yet you mingle with these people in the club, in business, in your home in a friendly way. You meet them every week, some of them every day, and you never speak to them on the subject of religion; you never bring it to their attention at all; you should be up and doing something for God and God's truth. There are always opportunities for a Christian to work for God. There is always a chance to speak to some one about God. Where you find one that won't care, you'll find one thousand that will.

The Dignity of Personal Work

If it is beneath your dignity to do personal work then you are above your Master. If you are not willing to do what He did, then don't call Him your Lord. The servant is not greater than the owner of the house. The chauffeur is not greater than the owner of the automobile. The servant on the railroad is not greater than the owners of the road. Certainly they are not greater than our Lord Jesus Christ.

It requires an effort to win souls to Christ. There is no harder work and none brings greater results than winning souls.

You will need courage. It is hard to do personal work and the devil will try to oppose you. You'll seek excuses to try and get out of it. Many people who attend the meetings regularly now will begin to stay at home when asked to do personal work. It will surprise you to know some lie to get out of doing personal work.

Personal work is the department of the church efficient to deal with the individual and not the masses. It is analogous to the sharpshooter in an army so dreaded by the opposing forces. The sharpshooter picks out the pivotal individual instead of shooting at the mass. The preacher shoots with a siege gun at long range. You can go to the individual and dispose of his difficulties. I shoot out there two or three hundred feet and you sit right beside people. If I were a physician and you were sick I would not prescribe en masse, I'd go and see you individually. I'd try to find out what was the matter and prescribe what you needed. Medicine is good for something, but not for everything.

The Privilege of Personal Work

Personal work is a great privilege. Not that God needs us, but that we need Him. Jesus Christ worked. "I must do the works of him that sent me." So must you. He didn't send me to work and you to loaf. Honor the God that gives you the privilege to do what He wants. Jesus worked.

Please God and see how it will delight your soul. If you'll win a soul you will have a blessing that the average church member knows nothing about. They are absolute strangers to the higher Christian life. We need an aroused church. A concerned church makes anxious sinners.

Who is wise? You say Andrew Carnegie, the millionaire was wise, the mayor, the judge, the governor, the educator, the superintendent of schools, the principal of the high school, the people who don't worry or don't live for pleasure, the inventor. What does the Lord say? The Lord says, "He who winneth souls is wise."

CHAPTER 21

"A GOOD SOLDIER OF
JESUS CHRIST"

*I'd rather undertake to save ten drunkards than
one old financial Shylock—it would be easier—*
"BILLY" SUNDAY.

SYMPATHETIC OBSERVERS COMMENTED in distressed
tones upon the physical exhaustion of Mr. Sunday after his addresses. He spoke with such intensity and vigor that he was completely spent by every
effort. To one who does not know that he worked
at this terrific pace for near a score of years it seemed
as if the evangelist was on the verge of a complete
collapse. He certainly seemed to speak "as a dying
man to dying men." The uttermost ounce of his
energy was offered up to each audience. "Billy"
Sunday was an unsparing worker.

For a month or six weeks of every year he gave
himself to rest. The remainder of the year he was
under a strain more intense than that of a great
political campaign. Even his Monday rest day,
which was supposed to be devoted to recuperation,
was oftener than not given to holding special meet-

ings in some other city than the one where he was
campaigning. Speaking twice or oftener every day,
to audiences averaging many thousands, is a tax
upon one's nerve force and vitality beyond all com-
putation. In addition to this, Sunday had his ad-
ministrative work, with its many perplexities and
grave responsibilities.

The evangelist, like every other man pre-eminent
in his calling, suffered a great loneliness; he had few
intimates who could lead his mind apart from his
work. What says Kipling, in his "Song of Diego
Valdez," the lord high admiral of Spain, who pined
in vain for the comradeship of old companions, but
who, in the aloneness of eminence, mourned his
solitary state?

> They sold Diego Valdez
> To bondage of great deeds.

The computable aggregate of Sunday's work is
almost unbelievable. His converts numbered about
four hundred thousand persons. That is a greater
total than the whole membership of the entire
Christian church decades after the resurrection of
our Lord. Imagine a city with this number of inhabitants, every one of whom was a zealous disciple
of Jesus Christ. What a procession these "trail-
hitters" would make.

When it came to counting up the aggregate size
of Sunday's audiences, one was tempted not to believe the figures, for the total ran up into the millions. Probably no man had ever before spoken to
so great numbers of human beings as "Billy" Sunday.

In point of conversions, as well as in many other
respects, "Billy" Sunday's most notable campaign
was that held in Boston, lasting ten weeks, in the
winter of 1916-17. The "trail-hitters" numbered
63,716, over 20,000 more than the number in Phil-

adelphia, which had previously held the record with 41,724 conversions. While these figures were to a certain extent a criterion by which to estimate the results of the Boston campaign, they were by no means its final measure. That 63,716 persons should have responded to "Billy" Sunday's invitation is something not lightly to be passed over. But the whole campaign, as other campaigns, served to draw particular attention to the church and its place in the community, and to lay emphasis upon the things for which the church stands.

CHAPTER 22

A WONDERFUL DAY AT A GREAT UNIVERSITY

The higher you climb the plainer you are seen—
"BILLY" SUNDAY.

BILLY" SUNDAY had many great days in his life—
mountain-top experiences of triumphant service; exalted occasions when it would seem that the
climax of his ministry had been reached. Doubtless,
though, the greatest day of his crowded life was the
thirtieth of March, 1914, which he spent with the
students of the University of Pennsylvania at Philadelphia.

The interest not alone of a great university but
also of a great city was concentrated upon him. An
imposing group of discriminating folk took the opportunity to judge the much discussed evangelist
and his work. In this respect, the day may be said
to have proved a turning point in the public career
of the evangelist. It silenced much of the wide-
spread criticism which had been directed toward

him up to the time; and it won for him the encomiums of a host of intellectual leaders.

What Sunday's own impressions of that day were may be understood from the prayer he offered at the close of the night meeting.

> Oh, Jesus, isn't this a fine bunch? Did you ever look down on a finer crowd? I don't believe there is a mother who is any prouder of this lot of boys than I am tonight. I have never preached to a more appreciative crowd, and if I never preach another sermon, I am willing to go Home to glory tonight, knowing that I have helped save the boys at the University of Pennsylvania. Help them to put aside temptations, and to follow in the paths in which Doctor Smith is trying to guide their feet.

Back of the visit of the evangelist to the University lies a story, and a great principle. The latter is that materialism has no message for the human soul or character. The authorities of the University, in common with a wide public, had been deeply disturbed over the suicide of several students during the winter of 1913-14. Sensational stories, largely unwarranted, in the daily press reported an epidemic of suicides, due to infidelity.

Underneath all this "yellow" portrayal of conditions lay the truth, realized by nobody more clearly than by the University head, Provost Edgar Fahs Smith, that the character of young manhood needs to be fortified by spiritual ideals. In his role of religious leader of the University, and counselor to the young men, Provost Smith had heard confessions of personal problems which had wrung his soul. None knew better than he that it takes more than culture to help a man win the battle of life. Looking in every direction for succor in this deepest of all problems, the sight of "Billy" Sunday at Scranton indicated a possible ray of hope.

Led by Thomas S. Evans, the secretary of the Christian Association of the University, a deputation of student leaders went to Scranton, heard the evangelist, and conveyed to him an invitation to spend a day with the University. The call of the need of young men in particular was irresistible to Sunday, and he gladly accepted the invitation for a day in Philadelphia—going, it may be added parenthetically, entirely at his own expense, and insisting that the offering made be devoted to University Christian Association work.

There was a thorough organization of the Christian work of the University; so careful plans were laid for the visit of the evangelist. The meetings were made the subject of student prayer groups, and all that forethought could do to secure the smooth running of the day's services was carefully attended to. Students were to be admitted by their registration cards, and a few hundred other guests, mostly ministers and persons identified with the University, were given special admission cards.

There is no such rush for grand opera tickets in Philadelphia as was experienced for these coveted cards of admission to the "Billy" Sunday meetings at the University. The noon meeting and the night meetings were exclusively for men, but in the afternoon a few score favored women were admitted. The result was that in these three services the evangelist talked to representatives of the best life of the conservative old city of Philadelphia. He never before had faced so much concentrated culture as was represented that day within the walls of the great gymnasium.

This improvised auditorium could be made to hold about three thousand persons, especially when the hearers were students, and skillful in crowding and utilizing every inch of space, such as window sills and rafters. The line of ticket holders that gathered before the opening of the doors itself preached a sermon to the whole city. As one of the Philadelphia newspapers remarked, in the title it gave to a section of its whole page of "Billy" Sunday pictures, "Wouldn't think they were striving for admittance to a religious service, would you?" The newspapers, by pen and camera, chronicled this "Billy" Sunday day at the University as the city's most important news for that issue.

The evangelist's chorister, Homer Rodeheaver, led the introductory service of music. He set the college boys to singing and whistling familiar gospel hymns, and Mrs. De Armond's "If Your Heart Keeps Right"—a refrain which was heard for many weeks afterward in University corridors and campus.

From the first the students, than whom there are no more critical hearers alive, were won by "Billy" Sunday. Provost Smith, who had the men's hearts, introduced him in this happy fashion:

" 'Billy' Sunday is a friend of men. He is a friend of yours and a friend of mine, and that's why we are glad to have him here today to tell us about his other friend, Jesus Christ. His is the spirit of friendship, and we are glad to extend to him our fellowship while we have the opportunity."

The three addresses given on that day were "What Shall I Do with Jesus?" "Real Manhood," and "Hot-cakes off the Griddle."

These fragments of the three addresses culled from the newspaper reports give the flavor of the messages heard by the students:

"Say, boys," Sunday demanded, leaning far over the platform, "are you fellows willing to slap Jesus Christ in the face in order to have some one come up and slap you on the back and say you are a good fellow and a dead-game sport? That is the surest way to lose out in life. I am giving you the experience of a life that knows.

"Pilate had his chance and he missed it. His name rings through the ages in scorn and contempt because he had not the courage to stand up for his convictions and Jesus Christ. Aren't you boys doing the same thing? You are convinced that Jesus Christ is the son of God, but you are afraid of the horse-laugh the boys will give you.

"God will have nothing to do with you unless you are willing to keep clean. Some people think they are not good enough to go to Heaven and not bad enough to go to Hell, and that God is too good to send them to Hell, so they fix up a little religion of their own. God isn't keeping any half-way house for any one. The man who believes in that will change his theology before he has been in Hell five minutes.

"There's just one enemy that keeps every one from accepting Christ, and that is your stubborn, miserable will power. You are not men enough to come clean for Jesus.

"I don't care whether you have brains enough to fill a hogshead or little enough to fill a thimble, you are up against this proposition: You must begin to measure Christ by the rules of God instead of the rules of men. Put him in the God class instead of in the man class; judge Christ by His task and the work He performed, and see if He was only a man."

The University of Pennsylvania would be turning out bigger men than Jesus Christ, Mr. Sunday said, if Christ were not the Son of God. The conditions and the opportunities are so much greater in these days, that a real superman should be the product of our day if education, society, business, politics and these varied interests could produce such an one.

"Jesus Christ is just as well known today as old

Cleopatra, the flat-nosed enchantress of the Nile, was known hundreds and hundreds of years ago.

"Don't swell up like a poisoned pup and say that 'it doesn't meet with my stupendous intellectual conception of what God intended should be understood.' God should have waited until you were born and then called you into counsel, I suppose. Say, fellows, I don't like to think that there are any four-flushing, excess-baggage, lackadaisical fools like that alive today, but there are a few.

"On the square, now, if you want to find a man of reason, would you go down in the red-light district, where women are selling their honor for money, or through the beer halls or fan-tan joints? You don't find intellect there," he continued.

In contrast to these places, the evangelist described with remarkable accuracy and emotion the scenes surrounding the death of President McKinley and the burial ceremony at Canton, Ohio.

"When I came out of that court-house at Canton, I said: 'Thank God, I'm in good company, for the greatest men of my nation are on the side of Jesus Christ,'" he added. From the farthest corner of the auditorium there came a fervent "Amen," which found many repetitions in the brief silence that followed.

Mr. Sunday reached a powerful climax when he described the possibilities of the judgment day, and the efforts of the evil one to lead into the dark, abysmal depths the souls of men who have been popular in the world. To those who have accepted Christ, the Saviour will appear on that day as an advocate at the heavenly throne and the saved ones can turn to the devil and say:

"'Beat it, you old skin-flint. I have you skinned to a frazzle. I have taken Jesus Christ and He's going to stand by me through all eternity.'

"Wherein does Jesus Christ fail to come up to your standard and the highest conception of the greatest Godlike spirit? Show me one flaw in His character. I challenge any infidel on earth to make good his claims that Christ was an ordinary man. The name of Jesus Christ, the son of God, is greater than any. It is the name that unhorsed Saul of Tarsus, and it is holding 500,000,000 of people by its majestic spell and enduring power.

"If you can't understand what this means, just take a walk out into some cemetery some day and look at the tombstones. You'll find that the name of the man who had a political drag twenty-five years ago is absolutely forgotten.

"Do you fellows know what sacrifice means?" suddenly asked Mr. Sunday. "Some of your fathers are making sacrifices and wearing old clothes just to keep you in school. He wants you to have an education because he can't even handle the multiplication table.

"If Jesus Christ should enter this gymnasium we would all fall to our knees. We have that much reverence in our hearts for Him. I would run down and meet Him, and would tell Him how much I love Him and that I am willing to go wherever He would have me go."

In closing, the evangelist told the story of a man who recklessly tossed a valuable pearl high into the air, reaching over the side of a ship to catch it as it fell. Time and again he was successful, but finally the ship swerved to one side and the gem disappeared beneath the waves.

"Boys, that man lost everything just to gain the plaudits of the crowd. Are you doing the same thing?

"That is the condition of thousands of people beneath the stars and stripes today—losing everything just to hear the clamor of the people, and get a little pat on the back for doing something the mob likes."

Mr. Sunday suddenly abandoned his dramatic attitude, and lowered his voice. There was an instantaneous bowing of heads, although he had given no suggestion of a prayer. It seemed proper at that time, and one of the evangelist's heart-to-heart talks with Christ, asking a blessing on the Christian workers of the University, and an earnest effort, on the part of every student, to live a Christian life, accompanied the great audience as it filed from the gymnasium.

*　　　*　　　*

When the invitation was given after the night meeting, for men who wanted to dedicate themselves to cleaner, nobler manhood to rise, nearly the entire body, visibly moved by the words of the preacher, rose. Then, with a daring which prim and conservative Philadelphia had not thought possible in this citadel of intellectuality and conventionality, Sunday gave the invitation to the students who would begin a new life by confessing Christ to come forward. Accounts vary as to the number who went up and grasped the evangelist's hand. All reporters seemed to be carried away by the thrill of the occasion. Many reported that hundreds went forward. The most conservative report was that 175 young men took this open stand of confession of Jesus Christ.

The University weekly, *Old Penn,* in its issue of the following Saturday summarized the "Billy" Sunday visit in pages of contributions. These three paragraphs are the sober judgment of those best informed from the University standpoint:

The results of Mr. Sunday's visit within the University have been nothing short of marvelous. The Provost has been receiving congratulations from trustees, businessmen, lawyers, members of the faculty and prominent undergraduates. Several whole fraternities have taken action leading to higher living in every line. Drink has been completely excluded from class banquets. Students are joining the churches, and religion has been the paramount topic of conversation throughout the entire University.

Under the leadership of the University Christian Association, the church leaders of Philadelphia of all denominations have been canvassing their own students in the University and have found most hearty response to everything that has to do with good living. The effect is really that of a religious crusade, and the result is of that permanent sort which expresses itself in righteousness of life. At the close of the night meeting on Monday, about 1,000 students arose to their feet in answer to Mr. Sunday's invitation to live the Christian life in earnest, or to join for the first time the Christian way of life. Those who have called upon the students who took this stand have found that it was genuine, and not in any sense due to a mere emotional movement. Mr. Sunday's appeal seems to be almost wholly to the will and conscience, but it is entirely based upon the movement of the Holy Spirit of God.

No one who has ever addressed the students of the University of Pennsylvania on vital religion has ever approached the success which was attained by Mr. Sunday in reaching the students, and without doubt this visit is only the opening up of a marvelous opportunity for Mr. Sunday to reach the students of the entire country, especially those of our great cosmopolitan universities.

The editor of *Old Penn* asked opinions from members of the faculty and undergraduate body. Dean Edward C. Kirk, M.D., D.D.S., of the Dental Department, said in his appraisal of the Sunday visit:

If, as according to some of the critics, the impression that he has made is but temporary and the enthusiasm which he has created is only a momentary impulse; even so, the success of his accomplishment lies in the fact that he has produced results where others have failed to make a beginning. The University ought to have the uplifting force not only of a "Billy" Sunday, but a "Billy" Monday, Tuesday, Wednesday and every other day in the week.

Of the students who testified in print, one, a prominent senior, wrote:

Mr. Sunday awoke in me a realization of my evil practices and sins so forcefully that I am going to make a determined effort to give them up and to make amends for the past. From my many conversations with fellow students I find that this is what Mr. Sunday did. If he did not directly cause the student to come forward and take a stand, every student at least was aroused to think about this important question in a light that he had not seriously considered it in before. The undergraduate body, as a whole, is glad that Mr. Sunday came to Philadelphia.

A Christian worker from the Law School gave his opinion as follows:

I have been connected with the University of Pennsylvania for six years, and for the greater part of this time have been in close touch with the work of the Christian Association. The influence of the Association seems to be increasing constantly, but "Billy" Sunday accomplished in one day what the Association would be proud to have accomplished in one year. To my mind, Mr. Sunday's visit marks the beginning of a new epoch—the renaissance of religious work of the University.

The conclusion, of course, is that the old-time religion, the gospel of our fathers and our mothers, is still the deepest need of all sorts and conditions of men. The religion that saved the outcast in the gutter was adequate to redeem the man in the university.

"BILLY" SUNDAY'S TESTIMONY

"It is said of Napoleon that one day he was riding in review before his troops, when the horse upon which he sat became unmanageable, seized the bit in his teeth, dashed down the road and the life of the famous warrior was in danger. A private, at the risk of his life, leaped out and seized the runaway horse, while Napoleon, out of gratitude, raised in the stirrups, saluted and said, 'Thank you, captain.' The man said, 'Captain of what, sir?' 'Captain of my Life Guards, sir,' said Napoleon.

"The man stepped over to where the Life Guards were in consultation and they ordered him back into the ranks. He refused to go and issued orders to the officer, 'I am Captain of the Guards.' Thinking him insane, they ordered his arrest and were dragging him away, when Napoleon rode up and the man said, 'I am Captain of the Guards because the Emperor said so.' Napoleon arose and said, 'Yes, Captain of my Life Guards. Loose him, sir; loose him.'

"I am a Christian because God says so, and I did what he told me to do, and I stand on God's Word and if the Book goes down, I'll go down with it. If God goes down, I'll go with Him, and if there were any other kind of God, except that God, I would have been shipwrecked long ago. Twenty-seven years ago in Chicago I piled all I had, my reputation, my character, my wife, children, home; I staked my soul, everything I had, on the God of the Bible, and the Christ of that Bible, and I won."

APPENDIX

MR. SUNDAY'S FAMOUS "BOOZE"
SERMON

HERE WE HAVE ONE of the strangest scenes in all the Gospels. Two men, possessed of devils, confront Jesus, and while the devils are crying out for Jesus to leave them, he commands the devils to come out, and the devils obey the command of Jesus. The devils ask permission to enter into a herd of swine feeding on the hillside. This is the only record we have of Jesus ever granting the petition of devils, and he did it for the salvation of men.

Then the fellows that kept the hogs went back to town and told the peanut-brained, weasel-eyed, hog-jowled, beetle-browned, bull-necked lobsters that owned the hogs, that "a long-haired fanatic from Nazareth, named Jesus, has driven the devils out of some men and the devils have gone into the hogs, and the hogs into the sea, and the sea into the hogs, and the whole bunch is dead."

And then the fat, fussy old fellows came out to see Jesus and said that he was hurting their business. A fellow says to me, "I don't think Jesus Christ did a nice thing."

You don't know what you are talking about.

Down in Nashville, Tennessee, I saw four wagons going down the street, and they were loaded with stills, and kettles, and pipes.

"What's this?" I said.

159

"United States revenue officers, and they have been in the moonshine district and confiscated the illicit stills, and they are taking them down to the government scrap heap."

Jesus Christ was God's revenue officer. Now the Jews were forbidden to eat pork, but Jesus Christ came and found that crowd buying and selling and dealing in pork, and confiscated the whole business, and he kept within the limits of the law when he did it. Then the fellows ran back to those who owned the hogs to tell what had befallen them and those hog-owners said to Jesus: "Take your helpers and hike. You are hurting our business." And they looked into the sea and the hogs were bottom side up, but Jesus said, "What is the matter?"

And they answered, "Leave our hogs and go." A fellow says it is rather a strange request for the devils to make, to ask permission to enter into hogs. I don't know—if I was a devil I would rather live in a good, decent hog than in lots of men. If you will drive the hog out you won't have to carry slop to him, so I will try to help you get rid of the hog.

And they told Jesus to leave the country. They said: "You are hurting our business."

Interest in Manhood

"Have you no interest in manhood?"

"We have no interest in that; just take your disciples and leave, for you are hurting our business."

That is the attitude of the liquor traffic toward the Church, and State, and Government, and the preacher that has the backbone to fight the most damnable, corrupt institution that ever wriggled out of Hell and fastened itself on the public.

I am a temperance Republican down to my toes. Who is the man that fights the whisky business in the South? It is the Democrats! They have driven the business from Kansas, they have driven it from Georgia, and Maine and Mississippi and North Carolina and North Dakota and Oklahoma and Tennessee and West Virginia. And they have driven it out of 1,756 counties. And it is the rock-ribbed Democratic South that is fighting the saloon. They started this fight that is sweeping

like fire over the United States. You might as well try
and dam Niagara Falls with toothpicks as to stop the reform wave sweeping our land. The Democratic party of
Florida has put a temperance plank in its platform and
the Republican party of every state would nail that
plank in their platform if they thought it would carry
the election. It is simply a matter of decency and manhood, irrespective of politics. It is prosperity against
poverty, sobriety against drunkenness, honesty against
thieving, Heaven against Hell. Don't you want to see
men sober? Brutal, staggering men transformed into
respectable citizens? "No," said a saloonkeeper, "to hell
with men. We are interested in our business, we have
no interest in humanity."

After all is said that can be said upon the liquor traffic,
its influence is degrading upon the individual, the family,
politics and business, and upon everything that you
touch in this old world. For the time has long gone by
when there is any ground for arguments as to its ill
effects. All are agreed on that point. There is just one
prime reason why the saloon has not been knocked into
hell, and that is the false statement that "the saloons are
needed to help lighten the taxes." The saloon business
has never paid, and it has cost fifty times more than the
revenue derived from it.

Does the Saloon Help Business?

I challenge you to show me where the saloon has ever
helped business, education, church, morals or anything
we hold dear.

The wholesale and retail trade in Iowa pays every year
at least $500,000 in licenses. Then if there were no
drawback it ought to reduce the taxation twenty-five
cents per capita. If the saloon is necessary to pay the
taxes, and if they pay $500,000 in taxes, it ought to
reduce them twenty-five cents a head. But no, the whisky business has increased taxes $1,000,000 instead of re-
ducing them, and I defy any whisky man on God's dirt
to show me one town that has the saloon where the
taxes are lower than where they do not have the saloon.
I defy you to show me an instance.

Listen! Seventy-five per cent of our idiots come from
intemperate parents; eighty per cent of the paupers,

eighty-two per cent of the crime is committed by men under the influence of liquor; ninety per cent of the adult criminals are whisky-made. The Chicago *Tribune* kept track for ten years and found that 53,556 murders were committed by men under the influence of liquor.

Archbishop Ireland, the famous Roman Catholic, of St. Paul, said of social crime, that "seventy-five per cent is caused by drink, and eighty per cent of the poverty."

I go to a family and it is broken up, and I say, "What caused this?" Drink! I step up to a young man on the scaffold and say, "What brought you here?" Drink! Whence all the misery and sorrow and corruption? Invariably it is drink.

Five Points, in New York, was a spot as near like hell as any spot on earth. There are five streets that run to this point, and right in the middle was an old brewery and the streets on either side were lined with grog shops. The newspapers turned a searchlight on the district, and the first thing they had to do was to buy the old brewery and turn it into a mission.

The Parent of Crimes

The saloon is the sum of all villainies. It is worse than war or pestilence. It is the crime of crimes. It is the parent of crimes and the mother of sins. It is the appalling source of misery and crime in the land. And to license such an incarnate fiend of hell is the dirtiest, low-down, damnable business on top of this old earth. There is nothing to be compared to it.

The legislature of Illinois appropriated $6,000,000 in 1908 to take care of the insane people in the state, and the whisky business produces seventy-five per cent of the insane. That is what you go down in your pockets for to help support. Do away with the saloons and you will close these institutions. The saloons make them necessary, and they make the poverty and fill the jails and the penitentiaries. Who has to pay the bills? The landlord who doesn't get the rent because the money goes for whisky; the butcher and the grocer and the charitable person who takes pity on the children of drunkards, and the taxpayer who supports the insane asylums and other institutions, that the whisky business keeps full of human wrecks.

Do away with the cursed business and you will not have to put up to support them. Who gets the money? The saloon-keepers and the brewers, and the distillers, while the whisky fills the land with misery, and poverty, and wretchedness, and disease, and death, and damnation, and it is being authorized by the will of the sovereign people.

You say that "people will drink anyway." Not by my vote. You say, "Men will murder their wives anyway." Not by my vote. "They will steal anyway." Not by my vote. You are the sovereign people, and what are you going to do about it?

Let me assemble before your minds the bodies of the drunken dead, who crawl away "into the jaws of death, into the mouth of hell," and then out of the valley of the shadow of the drink let me call the appertaining motherhood, and wifehood, and childhood, and let their tears rain down upon their purple faces. Do you think that would stop the curse of the liquor traffic? No! No!

In these days when the question of saloon or no saloon is at the fore in almost every community, one hears a good deal about what is called "personal liberty." These are fine, large, mouth-filling words, and they certainly do sound first rate; but when you get right down and analyze them in the light of common old horse-sense, you will discover that in their application to the present controversy they mean just about this: "Personal liberty" is for the man who, if he has the inclination and the price, can stand up at a bar and fill his hide so full of red liquor that he is transformed for the time being into an irresponsible, dangerous, evil-smelling brute. But "personal liberty" is not for his patient, long-suffering wife, who has to endure with what fortitude she may his blows and curses; nor is it for his children, who, if they escape his insane rage, are yet robbed of every known joy and privilege of childhood, and too often grow up neglected, uncared for and vicious as the result of their surroundings and the example before them. "Personal liberty" is not for the sober, industrious citizen who from the proceeds of honest toil and orderly living, has to pay, willingly or not, the tax bills which pile up as a direct result of drunkenness, disorder and poverty, the items of which are written in the records of every police court and poor-house in the land; nor is "personal liberty" for the good woman who goes abroad in the town only at the risk of being shot down by some drink-crazed creature. This rant about "personal liberty" as an argument has no leg to stand upon.

The Economic Side

Now, in 1913 the corn crop was 2,373,000,000 bushels, and it was valued at $1,660,000,000. Secretary Wilson says that the breweries use less than two per cent; I will say that they use two per cent. That would make 47,000,000 bushels, and at seventy cents a bushel that would be about $33,000,000. How many people are there in the United States? Ninety millions. Very well, then, that is thirty-six cents per capita. Then we sold out to the whisky business for thirty-six cents apiece—the price of a dozen eggs or a pound of butter. We are the cheapest gang this side of hell if we will do that kind of business.

Now listen! Last year the income of the United States government, and the cities and towns and counties, from the whisky business was $350,000,000. That is putting it liberally. You say that's a lot of money. Well, last year the workingmen spent $2,000,000,000 for drink, and it cost $1,200,000,000 to care for the judicial machinery. In other words, the whisky business cost us last year $3,400,000,000. I will subtract from that the dirty $350,000,000 which we got, and it leaves $3,050,000,000 in favor of knocking the whisky business out on purely a money basis. And listen! We spend $6,000,000,000 a year for our paupers and criminals, insane, orphans, feeble-minded, etc., and eighty-two per cent of our criminals are whisky-made, and seventy-five per cent of the paupers are whisky-made. The average factory hand earns $450 a year, and it costs us $1,200 a year to support each of our whisky criminals. There are 326,000 enrolled criminals in the United States and 80,000 in jails and penitentiaries. Three-fourths were sent there because of drink, and then they have the audacity to say the saloon is needed for money revenue. Never was there a baser lie.

"But," says the whisky fellow, "we would lose trade; the farmer would not come to town to trade." You lie.

I am a farmer. I was born and raised on a farm and I have the malodors of the barnyard on me today. Yes, sir. And when you say that you insult the best class of men on God's dirt. Say, when you put up the howl that if you don't have the saloons the farmer won't trade—say, Mr. Whisky Man, why do you dump money into politics and back the legislatures into the corner and fight to the last ditch to prevent the enactment of county local option? You know if the farmers were given a chance they would knock the whisky business into hell the first throw out of the box. You are afraid. You have cold feet on the proposition. You are afraid to give the farmer a chance. They are scared to death of you farmers.

I heard my friend ex-Governor Hanly, of Indiana, use the following illustrations:

"Oh, but," they say, "Governor, there is another danger to the local option, because it means a loss of market to the farmer. We are consumers of large quantities of grain in the manufacture of our products. If you drive us out of business you strike down that market and it will create a money panic in this country, such as you have never seen, if you do that." I might answer it by saying that less than two per cent of the grain produced in this country is used for that purpose, but I pass that by. I want to debate the merit of the statement itself, and I think I can demonstrate in ten minutes to any thoughtful man, to any farmer, that the brewer who furnishes him a market for a bushel of corn is not his benefactor, or the benefactor of any man, from an economic standpoint. Let us see. A farmer brings to the brewer a bushel of corn. He finds a market for it. He gets fifty cents and goes his way, with the statement of the brewer ringing in his ears, that the brewer is the benefactor. But you haven't got all the factors in the problem, Mr. Brewer, and you cannot get a correct solution of a problem without all the factors in the problem. You take the farmer's bushel of corn, brewer or distiller, and you brew and distill from it four and one-half gallons of spirits. I don't know how much he dilutes them before he puts them on the market. Only the brewer, the distiller and God know. The man who drinks it doesn't, but if he doesn't dilute it at all, he puts on the market four and a half gallons of intoxicating liquor, thirty-six pints. I am not going to trace the thirty-six pints. It will take too long. But I want to trace three of them and I will give you no imaginary stories plucked from the brain of an excited orator. I will take instances from the judicial pages of the Supreme Court and the Circuit Court judges' reports in Indiana and in Illinois to make my case.

Tragedies Born of Drink

Several years ago in the city of Chicago a young man of good parents, good character, one Sunday crossed the street and entered a saloon, open against the law. He found there boon companions. There were laughter, song and jest and much drinking. After awhile, drunk, insanely drunk, his money gone, he was kicked into the street. He found his way across to his mother's home. He importuned her for money to buy more drink. She refused him. He seized from the sideboard a revolver and ran out into the street and with the expressed determination of entering the saloon and getting more drink, money or no money. His fond mother followed him into the street. She put her hand upon him in a loving restraint. He struck it from him in anger, and then his sister came and added her entreaty in vain. And then a neighbor, whom he knew, trusted and respected, came and put his hand on him in gentleness and friendly kindness, but in an insanity of drunken rage he raised the revolver and shot his friend dead in his blood upon the street. There was a trial; he was found guilty of murder. He was sentenced to life imprisonment, and when the little mother heard the verdict—a frail little bit of a woman—she threw up her hands and fell in a swoon. In three hours she was dead.

In the streets of Freeport, Illinois, a young man of good family became involved in a controversy with a lewd woman of the town. He went in a drunken frenzy to his father's home, armed himself with a deadly weapon and set out for the city in search of the woman with whom he had quarreled. The first person he met upon the public square in the city, in the daylight, in a place where she had a right to be, was one of the most refined and cultured women of Freeport. She carried in her arms her babe—motherhood and babyhood, upon the streets of Freeport in the day time, where they had a right to be—but this young man in his drunken insanity mistook her for the woman he sought and shot her dead upon the streets with her babe in her arms. He was tried and Judge Ferand, in sentencing him to life imprisonment said: "You are the seventh man in two years to be sentenced for murder while intoxicated."

In the city of Anderson, you remember the tragedy in the Blake home. A young man came home intoxicated, demanding money of his mother. She refused it. He seized from the wood box a hatchet and killed his mother and then robbed her. You remember he fled. The officer of the law pursued him and brought him back. An indictment was read to him charging him with the murder of the mother who had given him his birth, of her who had gone down into the valley of the shadow of death to give him life, of her who had looked down into his blue eyes and thanked God for his life. And he said, "I am guilty; I did it all." And Judge McClure sentenced him to life imprisonment.

Now I have followed probably three of the thirty-six pints of the farmer's product of a bushel of corn and the three of them have struck down seven lives, the three boys who committed the murders, the three persons who were killed and the little mother who died of a broken heart. And now, I want to know, my farmer friend, if this has been a good commercial transaction for you? You sold a bushel of corn; you found a market; you got fifty cents; but a fraction of this product struck down seven lives, all of whom would have been consumers of your products for their life expectancy. And do you mean to say that is a good economic transaction to you? That disposes of the market question until it is answered; let no man argue further.

More Economics

And say, my friends, New York City's annual drink bill is $365,000,000 a year, $1,000,000 a day. Listen a minute. That is four times the annual output of gold, and six times the value of all the silver mined in the United States. And in New York there is one saloon for every thirty families. The money spent in New York by

the working people for drink in ten years would buy
every working man in New York a home, allowing
$3,500 for house and lot. It would take fifty persons one
year to count the money in $1 bills, and they would
cover 10,000 acres of ground. That is what the people
in New York dump into the whisky hole in one year.
And then you wonder why there is poverty and crime,
and that the country is not more prosperous.

The whisky gang is circulating a circular about Kansas City, Kansas. I defy you to prove a statement in it.
Kansas City is a town of 100,000 population, and temperance went into effect July 1, 1905. Then they had
250 saloons, 200 gambling hells and 60 houses of ill
fame. The population was largely foreign, and inquiries
have come from Germany, Sweden and Norway, asking
the influence of the enforcement of the prohibitory law.

At the end of one year the president of one of the
largest banks in that city, a man who protested against
the enforcement of the prohibitory law on the ground
that it would hurt business, found that his bank deposits
had increased $1,700,000, and seventy-two per cent of
the deposits were from men who had never saved a cent
before, and forty-two per cent came from men who never
had a dollar in the bank, but because the saloons were
driven out they had a chance to save, and the people
who objected on the grounds that it would injure business found an increase of 209 per cent in building op-
erations; and, furthermore, there were three times as
many more people seeking investment, and court expenses decreased $25,000 in one year.

Who pays to feed and keep the gang you have in
jail? Why, you go down in your sock and pay for what
the saloon has dumped in there. They don't do it. Mr.
Whisky Man, why don't you go down and take a picture
of wrecked and blighted homes, and of insane asylums,
with gibbering idiots. Why don't you take a picture of
that?

At Kansas City, Kansas, before the saloons were
closed, they were getting ready to build an addition to
the jail. Now the doors swing idly on the hinges and
there is nobody to lock in the jails. And the commis-
sioner of the Poor Farm says there is a wonderful falling
off of old men and women coming to the Poor House,

because their sons and daughters are saving their money and have quit spending it for drink. And they had to employ eighteen new school teachers for 600 boys and girls, between the ages of twelve and eighteen, that had never gone to school before because they had to help a drunken father support the family. And they have just set aside $200,000 to build a new school house, and the bonded indebtedness was reduced $245,000 in one year without the saloon revenue. And don't you know another thing? In 1906, when they had the saloon, the population, according to the directory, was 89,655. According to the census of 1907 the population was 100,835, or an increase of twelve per cent in one year, without the grog-shop. In two years the bank deposits increased $3,930,000.

You say, drive out the saloon and you kill business—Ha! ha! "Blessed are the dead that die in the Lord."

I tell you, gentlemen, the American home is the dearest heritage "of the people, for the people, and by the people," and when a man can go from home in the morning with the kisses of wife and children on his lips, and come back at night with an empty dinner bucket to a happy home, that man is a better man, whether white or black. Whatever takes away the comforts of home—whatever degrades that man or woman—whatever invades the sanctity of the home, is the deadliest foe to the home, to church, to state and school, and the saloon is the deadliest foe to the home, the church and the state, on top of God Almighty's dirt. And if all the combined forces of Hell should assemble in conclave, and with them all the men on earth that hate and despise God, and purity, and virtue—if all the scum of the earth could mingle with the denizens of Hell to try to think of the deadliest institution to home, to church and state, I tell you, sir, the combined hellish intelligence could not conceive of or bring an institution that could touch the hem of the garment of the open licensed saloon to damn the home and manhood, and womanhood, and business and every other good thing on God's earth.

In the Island of Jamaica the rats increased so that they destroyed the crops, and they introduced a mongoose. They have three breeding seasons a year and there are twelve to fifteen in each brood, and they are deadly enemies of the rats. The result was that the rats disappeared and there was nothing more for the mongoose to feed upon, so they attacked the snakes, and the frogs, and the lizards that fed upon the insects, with the result that the insects increased and they stripped the gardens, eating up the onions and the lettuce and then the mongoose attacked the sheep and the cats, and the puppies, and the calves and the geese. Now Jamaica is spending thousands of dollars to get rid of the mongoose.

The Amercian Mongoose

The American mongoose is the open licensed saloon. It eats the carpets off the floor and the clothes from off your back, your money out of the bank, and it eats up character, and it goes on until at last it leaves a stranded wreck in the home, a skeleton of what was once brightness and happiness.

There were some men playing cards on a railroad train, and one fellow pulled out a whisky flask and passed it about, and when it came to the drummer he said, "No." "What," they said, "have you got on the water wagon?" and they all laughed at him. He said, "You can laugh if you want to, but I was born with an appetite for drink, and for years I have taken from five to ten glasses per day, but I was at home in Chicago not long ago and I have a friend who has a pawn shop there. I was in there when in came a young fellow with ashen cheeks and a wild look on his face. He came up trembling, threw down a little package and said, 'Give me ten cents.' And what do you think was in that package? It was a pair of baby shoes.

"My friend said, 'No, I cannot take them.'

" 'But,' he said 'give me a dime. I must have a drink.'

" 'No, take them back home, your baby will need them.'

"And the poor fellow said, 'My baby is dead, and I want a drink.' "

Boys, I don't blame you for the lump that comes up in your throat. There is no law, divine or human, that the saloon respects. Lincoln said, "If slavery is not wrong, nothing is wrong." I say, if the saloon, with its train of diseases, crime and misery, is not wrong, then nothing on earth is wrong. If the fight is to be won we need men

—men that will fight—the Church, Catholic and Protestant, must fight it or run away, and thank God she will not run away, but fight to the last ditch.

Who works the hardest for his money, the saloon man or you?

Who has the most money Sunday morning, the saloon man or you?

The saloon comes as near being a rat hole for a wage-earner to dump his wages in as anything you can find. The only interest it pays is red eyes and foul breath, and the loss of health. You can go in with money and you come out with empty pockets. You go in with character and you come out ruined. You go in with a good position and you lose it. You lose your position in the bank, or in the cab of the locomotive. And it pays nothing back but disease and damnation and gives an extra dividend in delirium tremens and a free pass to Hell. And then it will let your wife be buried in the potter's field, and your children go to the asylum, and yet you walk out and say the saloon is a good institution, when it is the dirtiest thing on earth. It hasn't one leg to stand on and has nothing to commend it to a decent man, not one thing.

"But," you say, "we will regulate it by high license." Regulate what by high license? You might as well try and regulate a powder mill in Hell. Do you want to pay taxes in boys, or dirty money? A man that will sell out to that dirty business I have no use for. See how absurd their arguments are. If you drink Bourbon in a saloon that pays $1,000 a year license, will it eat your stomach less than if you drink it in a saloon that pays $500 license? Is it going to have any different effect on you, whether the gang pays $500 or $1,000 license? No. It will make no difference whether you drink it over a mahogany counter or a pine counter—it will have the same effect on you; it will damn you. So there is no use talking about it.

In some insane asylums, do you know what they do? When they want to test some patient to see whether he has recovered his reason, they have a room with a faucet in it, and a cement floor, and they give the patient a mop and tell him to mop up the floor. And if he has sense enough to turn off the faucet and mop up the floor they will parole him, but should he let the faucet run, they know that he is crazy.

Well, that is what you are trying to do. You are trying to mop it up with taxes and insane asylums and jails and Keeley cures, and reformations. The only thing to do is to shut off the source of supply.

A man was delivering a temperance address at a fair grounds and a fellow came up to him and said: "Are you the fellow that gave a talk on temperance?"

"Yes."

"Well. I think that the managers did a dirty piece of business to let you give a lecture on temperance. You have hurt my business and my business is a legal one."

"You are right there," said the lecturer, "they did do a mean trick; I would complain to the officers" And he took up a premium list and said. "By the way, I see there is a premium of so much offered for the best horse and cow and butter. What business are you in?"

"I'm in the liquor business."

"Well, I don't see that they offer any premium for your business. You ought to go down and compel them to offer a premium for your business and they ought to offer on the list $25 for the best wrecked home, $15 for the best bloated bum that you can show, and $10 for the finest specimen of broken-hearted wife, and they ought to give $25 for the finest specimens of thieves and gamblers you can trot out. You can bring out the finest looking criminals. If you have something that is good trot it out. You ought to come in competition with the farmer, with his stock, and the fancy work, and the canned fruit."

The Saloon a Coward

As Dr. Howard said: "I tell you that the saloon is a coward. It hides itself behind stained-glass doors and opaque windows, and sneaks its customers in at a blind door, and it keeps a sentinel to guard the door from the officers of the law, and it marks its wares with false bills-of-lading, and offers to ship green goods to you and marks them with the name of wholesome articles of food so people won't know what is being sent to you. And so vile did that business get that the legislature of Indiana passed a law forbidding a saloon to ship goods without being properly labeled. And the United States Congress passed a law forbidding them to send whisky through the mails.

I tell you it strikes in the night. It fights under cover of darkness and assassinates the characters that it cannot damn, and it lies about you. It attacks defenseless womanhood and childhood. The saloon is a coward. It is a thief; it is not an ordinary court offender that steals your money, but it robs you of manhood and leaves you in rags and takes away your friends, and robs your family. It impoverishes your children and it brings insanity and suicide. It will take the shirt off your back. It will steal the coffin from a dead child and yank the last crust of bread out of the hand of the starving child; it will take the last bucket of coal out of your cellar, and the last cent out of your pocket, and will send you home bleary-eyed and staggering to your wife and children. It will steal the milk from the breast of the mother and leave her nothing with which to feed her infant. It will take the virtue from your daughter. It is the dirtiest, most low-down, damnable business that ever crawled out of the pit of Hell. It is a sneak, and a thief and a coward.

It has no faith in God; has no religion. It would close every church in the land. It would hang its beer signs on the abandoned altars. It would close every public school. It respects the thief and it esteems the blasphemer; it fills the prisons and the penitentiaries. It despises Heaven, hates love, scorns virtue. It tempts the passions. Its music is the song of a siren. Its sermons are a collection of lewd, vile stories. It wraps a mantle about the hope of this world and that to come. Its tables are full of the vilest literature. It is the moral clearing house for rot, and damnation, and poverty, and insanity, and it wrecks homes and blights lives today.

God's Worst Enemy

The saloon is a liar. It promises good cheer and sends sorrow. It promises health and causes disease. It promises prosperity and sends adversity. It promises happiness and sends misery. Yes, it sends the husband home with a lie on his lips to his wife; and the boy home with a lie on his lips to his mother; and it causes the employee to lie to his employer. It degrades. It is God's worst enemy and the devil's best friend. It spares neither youth nor old age. It is waiting with a dirty blanket for the baby to crawl into the world. It lies in wait for the unborn.

It cocks the highwayman's pistol. It puts the rope in the hands of the mob. It is the anarchist of the world and its dirty red flag is dyed with the blood of women and children. It sent the bullet through the body of Lincoln; it nerved the arm that sent the bullets through Garfield and William McKinley. Yes, it is a murderer. Every plot that was ever hatched against the government and law, was born and bred, and crawled out of the grogshop to damn this country.

I tell you that the curse of God Almighty is on the saloon. Legislatures are legislating against it. Decent society is barring it. The fraternal brotherhoods are knocking it out. The Masons and Odd Fellows, and the Knights of Pythias and the A. O. U. W. are closing their doors to the whisky sellers. They don't want you wriggling your carcass in their lodges. Yes, sir, I tell you, the curse of God is on it. It is on the down grade. It is headed for Hell, and, by the grace of God, I am going to give it a push, with a whoop, for all I know how. . . .

A man comes along and I ask: "Are you a drunkard?"

"Yes, I'm a drunkard."

"Where are you going?"

"I am going to Hell."

"Why?"

"Because the Good Book says: 'No drunkard shall inherit the kingdom of God,' so I am going to Hell."

Another man comes along and I ask: "Are you a church member?"

"Yes, I am a church member."

"Where are you going?"

"I am going to Heaven."

"Did you vote for the saloon?"

"Yes."

"Then you shall go to Hell."

If the man that drinks the whisky goes to Hell, the man that votes for the saloon that sold the whisky to him will go to Hell. If the man that drinks the whisky goes to Hell, and the man that sold the whisky to the men that drank it, goes to Heaven, then the poor drunkard will have the right to stand on the brink of eternal damnation and put his arms around the pillar of justice, shake his fist in the face of the Almighty and say, "Unjust! Unjust!" If you vote for the dirty business you ought to go to Hell as sure as you live, and I would like to fire the furnace.

Some fellow says, "Drive the saloon out and the buildings will be empty." Which would you rather have, empty buildings or empty jails, penitentiaries and insane asylums? You drink the stuff and what have you to say? You that vote for it, and you that sell it? Look at them painted on the canvas of your recollection.

The Gin Mill

What is the matter with this grand old country? I heard my friend, George Stuart, tell how he imagined that he walked up to a mill and said:

"Hey, what kind of a mill are you?"

"A gin mill."

"I don't like the looks nor the smell of you. A gin mill; what do you make? What kind of a mill are you?"

"A gin mill."

"What is your raw material?"

"The boys of America."

The gin mills of this country must have 2,000,000 boys or shut up shop. Say, walk down your streets, count the homes and every fifth home has to furnish a boy for a drunkard. Have you furnished yours? No. Then I have to furnish two to make up.

"What is your raw material?"

"American boys."

"Then I will pick up the boys and give them to you."

A man says, "Hold on, not that boy, he is mine."

Then I will say to you what a saloon-keeper said to me when I protested, "I am not interested in boys; to Hell with your boys."

"Say, gin mill, what is your finished product?"

"Bleary-eyed, low-down, staggering men and scum of God's dirt."

Go to the jails, go to the insane asylums and the penitentiaries, and the homes for feeble-minded. There you will find the finished product for their dirty business.

I tell you it is the worst business this side of Hell, and you know it.

Here is an extract from the *Saturday Evening Post* of November 9, 1907, taken from a paper read by a brewer. You will say that a man didn't say it: "It appears from these facts that the success of our business lies in the creation of appetite among the boys. Men who have formed the habit scarcely ever reform, but they, like others, will die, and unless there are recruits made to take their places, our coffers will be empty, and I recommend to you that money spent in the creation of appetite will return in dollars to your tills after the habit is formed."

What is your raw material, saloons? American boys. Say, I would not give one boy for all the distilleries and saloons this side of Hell. And they have to have 2,000,000 boys every generation. And then you tell me you are a man when you will vote for an institution like that. What do you want to do, pay taxes in money or in boys? . . .

In a Northwest city a preacher sat at his breakfast table one Sunday morning. The doorbell rang; he answered it; and there stood a boy, twelve years of age. He was on crutches, right leg off at the knee, shivering, and he said, "Please, sir, will you come up to the jail and talk and pray with papa? He murdered mamma. Papa was good and kind, but whisky did it, and I have to support my three little sisters. I sell newspapers and black boots. Will you go up and talk and pray with papa? And will you come home and be with us when they bring him back? The governor says we can have his body after they hang him."

The preacher hurried to the jail and talked and prayed with the man. He had no knowledge of what he had done. He said, "I don't blame the law, but it breaks my heart to think that my children must be left in a cold and heartless world. Oh, sir, whisky did it."

The preacher was at the little hut when up drove the undertaker's wagon and they carried out the coffin. They led the little boy up to the coffin, he leaned over and kissed his father and sobbed, and said to his sisters, "Come on, sister, kiss papa's cheeks." And the little hungry, ragged, whisky orphans hurried to the coffin, shrieking in agony. Police, whose hearts were adamant, buried their faces in their hands and rushed from the house, and the preacher fell on his knees and lifted his clenched fist and tear-stained face and took an oath before God, and before the whisky orphans, that he would fight the cursed business until the undertaker carried him out.

A Chance for Manhood

You men have a chance to show your manhood. Then in the name of your mother, in the name of your manhood, in the name of your wife and the poor innocent children that climb up on your lap and put their arms around your neck, in the name of all that is good and noble, fight the curse. Shall you men, who hold in your hands the ballot, and in that ballot hold the destiny of womanhood and childhood and manhood, shall you, the sovereign power, refuse to rally in the name of the defenseless men and women and native land? No.

I want every man to say, "God, you can count on me to protect my wife, my home, my mother and my children and the manhood of America."

By the mercy of God, which has given to you the unshaken and unshakable confidence of her you love, I beseech you, make a fight for the women who wait until the saloons spew out their husbands and their sons, and send them home maudlin, brutish, devilish, stinking, blear-eyed, bloated-faced drunkards.

You say you can't prohibit men from drinking. Why, if Jesus Christ were here today some of you would keep on in sin just the same. But the law can be enforced against whisky just the same as it can be enforced against anything else, if you have honest officials to enforce it. Of course it doesn't prohibit. There isn't a law on the books of the state that prohibits. We have laws against murder. Do they prohibit? We have laws against burglary. Do they prohibit? We have laws against arson, rape, but they do not prohibit. Would you introduce a bill to repeal all the laws that do not prohibit? Any law will prohibit to a certain extent if honest officials enforce it. But no law will absolutely prohibit. We can make a law against liquor prohibit as much as any law prohibits.

Or would you introduce a bill saying, if you pay $1,000 a year you can kill any one you don't like; or by paying $500 a year you can attack any girl you want to; or by paying $100 a year you can steal anything that suits you? That's what you do with the dirtiest, rottenest gang this side of Hell. You say for so much a year you can have a license to make staggering, reeling, drunken sots, murderers and thieves and vagabonds. You say, "Bill, you're too hard on the whisky." I don't agree. Not on your life. . . .

Personal Liberty

Personal liberty is not personal license. I dare not exercise personal liberty if it infringes on the liberty of others. Our forefathers did not fight and die for personal license but for personal liberty bounded by laws. Personal liberty is the liberty of a murderer, a burglar, a seducer, or a wolf that wants to remain in a sheep fold, or the weasel in a hen roost. You have no right to vote for an institution that is going to drag your sons and daughters to Hell.

If you were the only person in this city you would have a perfect right to drive your horse down the street at breakneck speed; you would have a right to make a race track out of the streets for your auto; you could build a slaughter house in the public square; you could build a glue factory in the public square. But when the population increases from one to 600,000 you can't do it. You say, "Why can't I run my auto? I own it. Why can't I run my horse? I own it. Why can't I build the slaughter house? I own the lot." Yes, but there are 600,000 people here now and other people have rights.

So law stands between you and personal liberty. You can't build a slaughter house in your front yard, because the law says you can't As long as I am standing here on this platform I have personal liberty. I can swing my arms at will. But the minute any one else steps on the platform my personal liberty ceases. It stops just one inch from the other fellow's nose.

When you come staggering home, cussing right and left and spewing and spitting, your wife suffers, your children suffer. Don't think that you are the only one that suffers. A man that goes to the penitentiary makes his wife and children suffer just as much as he does. You're placing a shame on your wife and children. If you're a dirty, low-down, filthy, drunken, whisky-soaked bum you'll affect all with whom you come in contact. If you're a God-fearing man you will influence all with whom you come in contact. You can't live by yourself.

I occasionally hear a man say, "It's nobody's business how I live." Then I say he is the most dirty, low-down, whisky-soaked, beer-guzzling, bull-necked, foul-mouthed hypocrite that ever had a brain rotten enough to conceive such a statement and lips vile enough to utter it. You say, "If I am satisfied with my life why do you want to interfere with my business?"

If I heard a man beating his wife and heard her shrieks and the children's cries and my wife would tell me to go and see what was the matter, and I went in and found a great, big, broad-shouldered, whisky-soaked, hog-jowled, weasel-eyed brute dragging a little woman around by the hair, and two children in the corner unconscious from his kicks and the others yelling in abject terror, and he said, "What are you coming in to interfere with my personal liberty for? Isn't this my wife, didn't I pay for the license to wed her?" You ought, or you're a bigamist. "Aren't these my children; didn't I pay the doctor to bring them into the world?" You ought to, or you're a thief. "If I want to beat them, what is that your business, aren't they mine?" Would I apologize? Never! I'd knock seven kinds of pork out of that old hog.

The Moderate Drinker

I remember when I was secretary of the Y. M. C. A. in Chicago, I had the saloon route. I had to go around and give tickets inviting men to come to the Y. M. C. A. services. One day I was told to count the men going into a certain saloon. Not the ones already in, but just those going in. In sixty-two minutes I could count just 1,004 men going in there. I went in and met a fellow who used to be my side-kick out in Iowa, and he threw down a mint julep while I stood there, and I asked him what he was doing.

"Oh, just came down to the theater," he said, "and came over for a drink between acts."

"Why, you are three sheets in the wind now," I said, and then an old drunken bum, with a little threadbare coat, a straw hat, no vest, pants torn, toes sticking out through his torn shoes, and several weeks' growth of beard on his face, came in and said to the bartender: "For God's sake, can't you give an old bum a drink of whisky to warm up on?" and the bartender poured him out a big glass and he gulped it down. He pulled his hat down and slouched out.

I said to my friend, "George, do you see that old drunken bum, down and out? There was a time when he was just like you. No drunkard ever intended to be a drunkard. Every drunkard intended to be a moderate drinker."

"Oh, you're unduly excited over my welfare," he said. "I never expect to get that far."

"Neither did that bum," I answered. I was standing on another corner less than eight months afterward and I saw a bum coming along with head down, his eyes bloodshot, his face bloated, and he panhandled me for a flapjack before I recognized him. It was George. He had lost his job and was on the toboggan slide hitting it for Hell. I say if sin weren't so deceitful it wouldn't be so attractive. Every added drink makes it harder. . . .

By the grace of God I have strength enough to pass the open saloon, but some of you can't so I owe it to you to help you.

I've stood for more sneers and scoffs and insults and had my life threatened from one end of the land to the other by this God-forsaken gang of thugs and cutthroats because I have come out uncompromisingly against them. I've taken more dirty, vile insults from this low-down bunch than from any one on earth, but there is no one that will reach down lower, or reach higher up or wider, to help you out of the pits of drunkenness than I.

THE GOSPEL ACCORDING TO
SUNDAY

WHAT DOES CONVERTED MEAN.? It means completely changed. Converted is not synonymous with
reformed. Reforms are from without—conversion from
within. Conversion is a complete surrender to Jesus. It's
a willingness to do what he wants you to do. Unless you
have made a complete surrender and are doing His will
it will avail you nothing if you've reformed a thousand
times and have your name on fifty church records.

Believe on the Lord Jesus Christ in your heart and
confess Him with your mouth and you will be saved.
God is good. The plan of salvation is presented to you
in two parts. Believe in your heart and confess with
your mouth. Many of you here probably do believe.
Why don't you confess? Now own up. The truth is
that you have a yellow streak. Own up, businessmen,
and business women, and all of you others. Isn't it so?
Haven't you got a little saffron? Brave old Elijah ran
like a scared deer when he heard old Jezebel had said
she would have his head. He ran to Beersheba and lay
down under a juniper tree and cried to the Lord to let
him die. The Lord answered his prayer, but not in the
way he expected. If he had let him die he would have
died with nothing but the wind moaning through the
trees as his funeral dirge. But the Lord had something
better for Elijah. He had a chariot of fire and it swooped
down and carried him into glory without his ever seeing
death.

The Lord says He has something better for you—salvation—if He can get you to see it. You've kept your
church membership locked up. You've smiled at a

smutty story. When God and the church were scoffed at you never peeped, and when asked to stand up you've sneaked out the back way and beat it. You're afraid and God despises a coward. You cannot be converted by thinking so and sitting still.

Maybe you're a drunkard, an adulterer, a prostitute, a liar; won't admit you are lost; are proud. Maybe you're even proud you're not proud, and Jesus has a time of it.

Jesus said: "Come to me," not to the church; to Me, not to a creed; to Me, not to a preacher; to Me, not to an evangelist; to Me, not to a priest; to Me, not to a pope; "Come to me and I will give you rest." Faith in Jesus Christ saves you, not faith in the church.

You can join church, pay your share of the preacher's salary, attend the services, teach Sunday school, return thanks and do everything that would apparently stamp you as a Christian—even pray—but you won't ever be a Christian until you do what God tells you to do.

That's the road, and that's the only one mapped out for you and for me. God treats all alike. He doesn't furnish one plan for the banker and another for the janitor who sweeps out the bank. He has the same plan for one that he has for another. It's the law—you may not approve of it, but that doesn't make any difference.

Salvation a Personal Matter

The first thing to remember about being saved is that salvation is a personal matter. "Seek ye the Lord"— that means every one must seek for himself. It won't do for the parent to seek for the children; it won't do for the children to seek for the parent. If you were sick, all the medicine I might take wouldn't do you any good. Salvation is a personal matter that no one else can do for you; you must attend to it yourself.

Some persons have lived manly or womanly lives, and they lack but one thing—open confession of the Lord Jesus Christ. Some men think that they must come to Him in a certain way—that they must be stirred by emotion or something.

Some people have a deeper conviction of sin before they are converted than after they are converted. With some it is the other way. Some know when they are converted and others do not.

Some people are emotional. Some are demonstrative. Some will cry easily. Some are cold and can't be moved to emotion. A man jumped up in a meeting and asked whether he could be saved when he hadn't shed a tear in forty years. Even as he spoke he began to shed tears. It's all a matter of how you're constituted. I am vehement, and I serve God with the same vehemence that I served the devil when I went down the line.

Some of you say that in order to accept Jesus you must have different surroundings. You think you could do it better in some other place. You can be saved where you are as well as any place on earth. I say, "My watch doesn't run. It needs new surroundings. I'll put it in this other pocket, or I'll put it here, or here on these flowers." It doesn't need new surroundings. It needs a new mainspring; and that's what the sinner needs. You need a new heart, not a new suit.

What can I do to keep out of Hell? "Believe on the Lord Jesus Christ and thou shalt be saved."

The Philippian jailer was converted. He had put the disciples into the stocks when they came to the prison, but after his conversion he stooped down and washed the blood from their stripes.

Now, leave God out of the proposition for a minute. Never mind about the new birth—that's His business. Jesus Christ became a man, bone of our bone, flesh of our flesh. He died on the cross for us, so that we might escape the penalty pronounced on us. Now, never mind about anything but our part in salvation. Here it is: "Believe on the Lord Jesus Christ, and thou shalt be saved."

You say, "Mr. Sunday, the church is full of hypocrites." So's Hell. I say to you if you don't want to go to Hell and live with that bunch forever, come into the church, where you won't have to associate with them very long. There are no hypocrites in Heaven.

You say, "Mr. Sunday, I can be a Christian and go to Heaven without joining a church." Yes, and you can go to Europe without getting on board a steamer. The swimming's good—but the sharks are laying for fellows who take that route. I don't believe you. If a man is truly saved he will hunt for a church right away.

You say, "It's so mysterious. I don't understand."

You'll be surprsied to find out how little you know. You plant a seed in the ground; that's your part. You don't understand how it grows. How God makes that seed grow is mysterious to you.

Some people think that they can't be converted unless they go down on their knees in the straw at a camp meeting, unless they pray all hours of the night, and all nights of the week, while some old brother storms Heaven in prayer. Some think a man must lose sleep, must come down the aisle with a haggard look; he must froth at the mouth and dance and shout. Some get it that way, and they don't think that the work I do is genuine unless conversions are made in the same way.

I want you to see what God put in black and white; that there can be a sound, thorough conversion in an instant; that man can be converted as quietly as the coming of day and never backslide. I do not find fault with the way other people get religion. What I want and preach is the fact that a man can be converted without any fuss.

If a man wants to shout and clap his hands in joy over his wife's conversion, or if a wife wants to cry when her husband is converted, I am not going to turn the hose on them, or put them in a strait-jacket. When a man turns to God truly in conversion, I don't care what form his conversion takes. I wasn't converted that way, but I do not rush around and say, with gall and bitterness, that you are not saved because you did not get religion the way I did. If we all got it in the same way, the devil might go to sleep with a regular Rip Van Winkle snooze and still be on the job.

You could never get a man with the temperament of Nicodemus near a camp meeting, to kneel down in the straw, or to shout and sing. He was a quiet, thoughtful, honest, sincere and cautious man. He wanted to know the truth and he was willing to walk in the light when he found it.

Look at the man at the pool of Bethesda. He was a big sinner and was in a lot of trouble which his sins had made for him. He had been in that condition for a long time. It didn't take him three minutes to say "Yes," when the Lord spoke to him. See how quietly he was converted: "And he arose and followed him."

Matthew stood in the presence of Christ; he realized what it would be to be without Christ, to be without hope, and it brought him to a quick decision. "And he arose and followed him."

How long did that conversion take? How long did it take him to accept Christ after he had made up his mind? And you tell me you can't make an instant decision to please God? The decision of Matthew proves that you can. While he was sitting at his desk he was not a disciple. The instant he arose he was. That move changed his attitude toward God. Then he ceased to do evil and commenced to do good. You can be converted just as quickly as Matthew was.

God says: "Let the wicked forsake his way." The instant that is done, no matter if the man has been a lifelong sinner, he is safe. There is no need of struggling for hours—or for days—do it now. Who are you struggling with? Not God. God's mind was made up long before the foundations of the earth were laid. The plan of salvation was made long before there was any sin in the world. Electricity existed long before there was any car wheel for it to drive. "Let the wicked forsake his way." When? Within a month, within a week, within a day, within an hour? No! Now! The instant you yield, God's plan of salvation is thrown into gear. You will be saved before you know it, like a child being born.

Rising and following Christ switched Matthew from the broad to the narrow way. He must have counted the cost as he would have balanced his cash book. He put one side against the other. The life he was living led to all chance of gain. On the other side there was Jesus, and Jesus outweighs all else. He saw the balance turn as the tide of a battle turns and then it ended with his decision. The sinner died and the disciple was born.

I believe that the reason the story of Matthew was written was to show how a man could be converted quickly and quietly. It didn't take him five or ten years to begin to do something—he got busy right away.

You don't believe in quick conversions? There have been a dozen men of modern times who have been powers for God whose conversions were as quiet as Matthew's. Charles G. Finney never went to a camp meeting. He was out in the woods alone, praying, when he was converted. Sam Jones, a mighty man of God, was converted at the bedside of his dying father. Moody accepted Christ while waiting on a customer in a boot and shoe store. Dr. Chapman was converted as a boy in a Sunday school. All the other boys in the class had accepted Christ, and only Wilbur remained. The teacher turned to him and said, "And how about you, Wilbur?" He said, "I will," and he turned to Christ and has been a most powerful evangelist for many years. Gipsy Smith was converted in his father's tent. Torrey was an agnostic, and in comparing agnosticism, infidelity and Christianity, he found the scale tipped toward Christ.

Seemingly the men who have moved the world for Christ have been converted in a quiet manner. The way to judge a tree is by its fruit. Judge a tree of quiet conversion in this way.

When conversion compels people to forsake their previous calling, God gives them a better job. Luke said, "He left all." Little did he dream that his influence would be world-reaching and eternity-covering. His position as tax collector seemed like a big job, but it was picking up pins compared to the job God gave him. Some of you may be holding back for fear of being put out of your job. If you do right God will see that you do not suffer. He has given plenty of promises, and if you plant your feet on them you can defy the poorhouse. Trust in the Lord means that God will feed you. Following Christ you may discover a gold mine of ability that you never dreamed of possessing. There was a saloon keeper, converted in a meeting at New Castle, who won hundreds of people to Christ by his testimony and his preaching.

You do not need to be in the church before the voice comes to you; you don't need to be reading the Bible; you don't need to be rich or poor or learned. Wherever Christ comes, follow. You may be converted while engaged in your business. Men cannot put up a wall and keep Jesus away. The still small voice will find you.

At the Crossroads

Right where the two roads through life diverge God has put Calvary. There He put up a cross, the stumbling block over which the love of God said, "I'll touch the heart of man with the thought of father and son." He thought that would win the world to him, but for nineteen hundred years men have climbed the Mount of Calvary and trampled into the earth the tenderest teachings of God.

You are on the devil's side. How are you going to cross over?

So you cross the line and God won't issue any extradition papers. Some of you want to cross. If you believe, then say so, and step across. There are hundreds that are on the edge of the line and many are standing straddling it. But that won't save you. You believe in your heart—confess Him with your mouth. With his heart man believes and with his mouth he confesses. Then confess and receive salvation full, free, perfect and external. God will not grant any extradition papers. A man isn't a soldier because he wears a uniform, or carries a gun, or carries a canteen. He is a soldier when he makes a definite enlistment. All of the others can be bought without enlisting. When a man becomes a soldier he goes out on muster day and takes an oath to defend his country. It's the oath that makes him a soldier. Going to church doesn't make you a Christian any more than going to a garage makes you an automobile, but public definite enlistment for Christ makes you a Christian.

"Oh," a woman said to me out in Iowa, "Mr. Sunday, I don't think I have to confess with my mouth." I said: "You're putting up your thought against God's."

M-o-u-t-h doesn't spell intellect. It spells mouth and you must confess with your mouth. The mouth is the biggest part about most people, anyhow.

What must I do?

Philosophy doesn't answer it. Infidelity doesn't answer it. First, "believe on the Lord Jesus Christ and thou shalt be saved." Believe on the Lord. Lord—that's His kingly name. That's the name He reigns under. "Thou shalt call his name Jesus." It takes that kind of a confession. Give me a Saviour with a sympathetic eye to watch me so I shall not slander. Give me a Saviour with a strong arm to catch me if I stumble. Give me a Saviour that will hear my slightest moan.

Believe on the Lord Jesus Christ and be saved. Christ

is His resurrection name. He is sitting at the right hand
of the Father interceding for us.

Because of His divinity He understands God's side of
it and because of His humanity He understands our
side of it. Who is better qualified to be the mediator?
He's a Mediator. What is that? A lawyer is a mediator
between the jury and the defendant. A retail merchant
is a mediator between the wholesale dealer and the con-
sumer. Therefore, Jesus Christ is the Mediator between
God and man. Believe on the Lord. He's ruling today.
Believe on the Lord Jesus. He died to save us. Believe
on the Lord Jesus Christ. He's the Mediator.

Her majesty, Queen Victoria, was traveling in Scot-
land when a storm came up and she took refuge in a
little hut of a Highlander. She stayed there for an hour
and when she went the good wife said to her husband,
"We'll tie a ribbon on that chair because her majesty
has sat on it and no one else will ever sit on it." A friend
of mine was there later and was going to sit in the
chair when the man cried: "Nae, nae, mon. Dinna sit
there. Her majesty spent an hour with us once and she
sat on that chair and we tied a ribbon on it and no one
else will ever sit on it." They were honored that her
majesty had spent an hour with them. It brought un-
speakable joy to them.

It's great that Jesus Christ will sit on the throne of my
heart, not for an hour, but to sway His power forever
and ever.

"He Died for Me"

In the war there was a band of guerillas, Quantrell's
band, that had been ordered to be shot on sight. They
had burned a town in Iowa and they had been caught.
One long ditch was dug and they were lined up in front
of it and blindfolded and tied. Just as the firing squad
was ready to present arms a young man dashed through
the bushes and cried, "Stop!" He told the commander
of the firing squad that he was as guilty as any of the
others. He had escaped and had come of his own free
will, and pointing to one man in the line he asked to
take his place. "I'm single," he said, "while he has a
wife and babies." The commander of that firing squad
was an usher in one of the cities in which I held meet-

ings, and he told me how the young fellow was blind-folded and bound and the guns rang out and he fell dead.

Time went on and one day a man came upon another in a graveyard in Missouri weeping and shaping the grave into form. The first man asked who was buried there and the other said, "The best friend I ever had." Then he told how he had not gone far away but had come back and taken the body of his friend after he had been shot. He buried it; so he knew he had the right body. And he had brought a withered bouquet all the way from his home to put on the grave. He was poor then and could not afford anything costly, but he had placed a slab of wood on the pliable earth with these words on it: "He died for me."

Major Whittle stood by the grave some time later and saw the monument. The man became rich and today there is a marble monument fifteen feet high and on it this inscription:

SACRED TO THE MEMORY OF
WILLIE LEE
HE TOOK MY PLACE IN THE LINE
HE DIED FOR ME

Sacred to the memory of Jesus Christ. He took our place on the cross and gave His life that we might live, and go to Heaven and reign with Him.

Believe on the Lord Jesus Christ, confess Him with your mouth, and you shall be saved and your house.

It is a great salvation that can reach down into the quagmire of filth, pull a young man out and send him out to hunt his mother and fill her days with sunshine. It is a great salvation, for it saves from great sin.

The way to salvation is not Harvard, Yale, Princeton, Vassar or Wellesley. Environment and culture can't put you into Heaven without you accepting Jesus Christ.

It's great. I want to tell you that the way to Heaven is a bloodstained way. No man has and never will reach it without Jesus Christ.